Praise for Robert B. Reich's

The System

"The themes [Reich] discusses eerily adumbrate our current circumstance and shed light on possible ways forward."

—*Forbes*

"An accessible and eminently readable walkthrough of thirty years of neoliberal fiscal policy, corporate malfeasance, and lobbying wickedness. The reader is left with a crystal-clear understanding of how democracy decays and the specific forces that have bled the middle-class dry, leaving us with an oligarchy in which the average citizen has virtually no power."

—*Salon*

"Reich does a brilliant job succinctly reminding us of the scale and scope of corporate corruption, economic inequality, and political spinelessness in America."

—*New York Journal of Books*

"[An] essential activist . . . preaching the truth amid all of the misinformation and short-sighted gains that infect our offices of power. . . . Robert Reich proves that clear-eyed community-minded thinking is still with us." —*Interview* magazine

"[*The System*] is ultimately an examination of the nature of power. Such an examination easily dispels the demagogic narrative, pulling back the curtain of wealth and power that currently obscures those with both from careful examination of how they secured and perpetuate such privilege. . . . For decades, [the market] has been serving fewer and fewer, and the only way to turn the tide back in the favor of the many is for citizens to re-engage and raise our voices."   —*Porchlight*

"A characteristically powerful and engaging study of inequality."
—*The Big Issue*

"Incisive. . . . His critique of the current system is evidence-based and authoritative. This call-to-action will resonate with progressive readers."   —*Publishers Weekly*

"[A] much-needed, readably concise political and economic analysis."   —*Kirkus Reviews*

Robert B. Reich

The System

Robert B. Reich is chancellor's professor of public policy at the Goldman School of Public Policy at the University of California, Berkeley. He has served in three national administrations and has written seventeen books, including *The Work of Nations*, *The Common Good*, *Saving Capitalism*, *Supercapitalism*, and *Locked in the Cabinet*. His articles have appeared in *The New Yorker*, *The Atlantic*, *The New York Times*, *The Washington Post*, and *The Wall Street Journal*, and he writes a weekly column for *The Guardian* and *Newsweek*. He is cocreator of the award-winning film *Inequality for All* and the Netflix original documentary *Saving Capitalism* and cofounder of Inequality Media. He lives in Berkeley and blogs at robertreich.org.

The System

The System

Who Rigged It, How We Fix It

Robert B. Reich

VINTAGE BOOKS

A Division of Penguin Random House LLC

New York

FIRST VINTAGE BOOKS EDITION, FEBRUARY 2021

Copyright © 2020 by Robert B. Reich

All rights reserved. Published in the United States by Vintage Books,
a division of Penguin Random House LLC, New York, and distributed
in Canada by Penguin Random House Canada Limited, Toronto.
Originally published in hardcover in the United States by
Alfred A. Knopf, a division of Penguin Random
House LLC, New York, in 2020.

Vintage and colophon are registered
trademarks of Penguin Random House LLC.

The Library of Congress has cataloged the Knopf edition as follows:
Name: Reich, Robert B., author.
Title: The system : who rigged it, how we fix it / Robert B. Reich.
Description: First edition. | New York : Alfred A. Knopf, 2020.
Identifiers: LCCN 2019044129
Subjects: LCSH: Dimon, Jamie. | Democracy—United States. |
Oligarchy—United States. | Corporate power—United States. | Business
and politics—United States. | Elite (Social sciences)—United States. |
United States—Politics and government—1989–.
Classification: LCC JK275 .R455 2020 | DDC 322/.30973—dc23
LC record available at https://lccn.loc.gov/2019044129

Vintage Books Trade Paperback ISBN: 978-0-593-08200-3
eBook ISBN: 978-0-525-65905-1

Author photograph © Delaney Inamine
Book design by Maggie Hinders

www.vintagebooks.com

Printed in the United States of America

10   9   8   7   6   5   4

For future generations

Contents

The System

Introduction

IN THE SPRING OF 2018, Jamie Dimon phoned me at my office at the University of California, Berkeley. I had criticized him publicly, and he was not pleased. He sounded off on the phone for several minutes without stopping. Finally he asked, "You still there?" I said, "Yes," and then told him in abbreviated form what I will tell you in the rest of this book.

Dimon has a great amount of influence over the system. He heads the largest bank on Wall Street, JPMorgan Chase, which survived the 2008 financial crisis better than any other big bank. After the crisis, *The New York Times* gave Dimon the backhanded compliment of being "America's least-hated banker." He also heads the Business Roundtable, a lobbying group of the most powerful CEOs in America. He is featured regularly on cable news and in the business press. His opinions carry significant weight on Capitol Hill.

Dimon describes himself as "a patriot before I'm the CEO of JPMorgan." He is a lifelong Democrat. He speaks out about the injustices and inequalities of contemporary America. He is not just talk. He has pushed his bank to invest in poor cities and to create better opportunities for the disadvantaged.

I believe he's sincere. But he is awash in self-delusion, a condition especially dangerous in people who have significant power over others. Dimon doesn't see how he has contributed to the mess we're in. He doesn't acknowledge the inconsistencies between his preferred self-image as "patriot first" and his roles as CEO of America's largest bank and chairman of the Business Roundtable. He doesn't understand how he has hijacked the system.

I often single out Dimon in this book because he is emblematic of an abdication of public responsibility to maintain the health of our political-economic system at a time when a comparative few at the top have more power over it than at any time in over a century. They have used their power to give themselves unprecedented wealth, which has bought them even more power. They have justified their wealth and power as being in the interest of the public, but the public has been shafted.

Dimon himself is not the problem. If he weren't running JPMorgan or chairing the Business Roundtable, someone else would be, and probably not as capably. Regardless of who is in charge, a big part of those jobs is siphoning off the gains of the economy for the benefit of a few at the top. This is how the current system is organized. This is how incentives within the system are designed.

To the extent Dimon or others like him are blameworthy, the fault lies in their unwillingness to buck these incentives in order to change the system for the well-being of the vast majority. This may be an unrealistically high bar. Dimon has no legal obligation to reach it. But does he have a moral duty to try to change the laws and incentives so no one ever again can become as rich and powerful as he and his colleagues at the Business Roundtable? Does he have a moral obligation to ensure that the American system is no longer rigged in favor of people like him? I believe he does. Let me explain.

Millions of Americans, whether on the left or right of the political spectrum, know something has gone profoundly wrong.

"Our system has been rigged against the American people," the Biden-Sanders Unity Task Force reported in 2020.

"Big business, elite media, and major donors are lining up behind the campaign of my opponent because they know she will keep our rigged system in place," said Donald Trump at the Republican convention in 2016 (the same year he paid $750 in taxes).

As *New York* magazine's Frank Rich put it: "Everything in the country is broken. Not just Washington, which failed to prevent the financial catastrophe and has done little to protect us from the next, but also race relations, health care, education, institutional religion, law enforcement, the physical infrastructure, the news media, the bedrock virtues of civility and community. Nearly everything has turned to crap, it seems, except

Peak TV (for those who can afford it)." He might have added a cataclysmic pandemic and a perilously weakened democracy.

Donald Trump is gone, but many of the underlying conditions that led to Trump have worsened. The increasing concentration of wealth and power at the top has created an education system in which the super-rich can buy admission to college for their children, a political system in which they can buy Congress and the presidency, an information ecosystem in which they can buy public opinion, a health-care system in which they can buy care others can't, and a justice system in which they can buy their way out of jail. Billionaires prospered even in the pandemic. Almost everyone else has been hurled into a dystopia of bureaucratic arbitrariness, corporate indifference, and the legal and financial sinkholes that have become hallmarks of modern American life.

Even in a post-Trump America, this mammoth, systemic dysfunction continues to generate a great deal of heat—anger, upset, frustration, and outrage. Heat in any system signals potential change. Like tectonic plates causing earthquakes and volcanoes as they crash into each other, heat is a sign of underlying tumult. In today's America, the status quo is unsustainable. Subterranean tensions are building.

The cast of characters in power may change with an election but the system remains firmly in place.

If you want to understand where the system is now and what you might do to help move it in a more humane direction, you will need to look under its surface and reassess many of your assumptions.

First, forget politics as you've come to see it as electoral contests between Democrats and Republicans. Think power. The underlying contest is between a small minority who have gained power over the system and the vast majority who have little or none.

Don't assume that a U.S. president or any other head of state unilaterally makes big decisions. Look at the people who enable and encourage those decisions, and whose interests those decisions serve.

Forget what you may have learned about the choice between the "free market" and government. A market cannot exist without a government to organize and enforce it. The important question is whom the market has been organized to serve.

Forget the standard economic goals of higher growth and greater efficiency. The issue is who benefits from more growth and efficiency.

Don't be dazzled by "corporate social responsibility." Most of it is public relations. Corporations won't voluntarily sacrifice shareholder returns unless laws require them to. Even then, be skeptical of laws unless they're enforced and backed by big penalties. Large corporations and the super-rich ignore laws when the penalties for violating them are small relative to the gains for breaking them. Fines are then simply very manageable costs of doing business.

Don't assume that we're locked in a battle between capitalism and socialism. We already have socialism—for the very rich. Most Americans are subject to harsh capitalism.

Don't define "national competitiveness" as the profitability of large American corporations. Those corporations are now global, with no allegiance to America. Real national competitiveness lies in the productivity of the American people—which depends on their education, health, and infrastructure linking them together.

You can also forget the ups and downs of the business cycle. Focus instead on systemic changes that have caused the wealth and power of a few to dramatically increase during the last forty years at the expense of the many.

Forget the old idea that corporations succeed by becoming better, cheaper, or faster than their competitors. They now succeed mainly by increasing their monopoly power.

Forget any traditional definition of finance. Think instead of a giant gambling casino in which bets are made on large flows of money, and bets are made on those bets (called derivatives). The biggest winners have better inside-information than anyone else.

Don't confuse attractive policy proposals with changes in the system as a whole. Even if enacted, such proposals at most mitigate systemic problems. Solving those systemic problems requires altering the allocation of power.

Don't assume society will fundamentally improve just because certain bad actors (including, say, a sociopathic president) are replaced by good ones. If systemic problems aren't addressed, nothing important will change.

Don't assume the system is stable. It moves through vicious spirals and virtuous cycles. We are now in a vicious spiral. The challenge is to turn the vicious into the virtuous.

Don't believe the system is a meritocracy in which ability and hard work are necessarily rewarded. Today the most important predictor of someone's future income and wealth is the income and wealth of the family they're born into.

Don't separate race from class. Racial discrimination is aggravating class divides, and wider inequality is worsening racial divides.

Think *systemically.* Most people's incomes haven't risen for four decades, and they are becoming less economically secure. Meanwhile, climate change is intensifying competition for arable land and potable water around the world, generating larger flows of refugees and immigrants. Dangerous viruses are also more likely to spread in places with poor air quality and poor people. Together these facts have allowed demagogues to blame stagnant incomes on immigrants and a pandemic on other nations and the poor.

Most importantly, you will need to understand the nature of power—who possesses it and why, how it is wielded, and for what purposes. Power is the ability to direct or influence the behavior of others. On a large scale, power is the capacity to set the public agenda—to frame big choices, to influence legislators, and to get laws enacted or prevent them from being enacted, to assert one's will on the world.

Power has been leached out of conventional discussions about what is occurring. Power doesn't show up in standard economics texts, finance courses, or even political science and law. But you cannot comprehend today's system without confronting power head on. It is the most important subterranean force.

Power is exercised through institutions—big Wall Street

banks, global corporations, the executive and legislative branches of government, the Federal Reserve and the Supreme Court, the military, elite universities, and the media (including social media as organized by Big Tech).

But these institutions don't wield power on their own. Particular people have outsized influence over them. They include CEOs such as Jamie Dimon, large investors, hedge fund and private equity managers, media moguls, key lobbying groups such as the Business Roundtable, and major donors to political candidates and universities. As the climate activist Greta Thunberg observes, "If everyone is guilty, then no one is to blame. And someone is to blame. Some people—some companies and some decision-makers in particular—have known exactly what priceless values they are sacrificing to continue making unimaginable amounts of money."

To comprehend the nature of their influence over the system, you'll need to understand the role of wealth. In the system we now have, power and wealth are inseparable. Great wealth flows from great power; great power depends on great wealth. Wealth and power have become one and the same.

I don't intend for these underlying realities to make you more cynical about the system or resigned to its intransigence. To the contrary, the first step toward changing the system is to understand it. If we cannot comprehend the truth, we become entrapped in conventional falsehoods and false choices, unable to envision new possibilities. Seeing the system for what it is will empower you to join with others to change it for the better.

PART I

Democracy vs. Oligarchy

CHAPTER 1

The Obsolescence of Right and Left

A HALF CENTURY AGO, when America had a large and grow-ing middle class, those on the "left" wanted stronger social safety nets and more public investment in schools, roads, and research. Those on the "right" sought greater reliance on the free market. But as power and wealth have moved to the top, everyone else—whether on the old right or the old left—has become disempowered and less secure. Today the great divide is not between left and right. It's between democracy and oligarchy.

The word "oligarchy" comes from the Greek word *oligarkhes,* meaning "few to rule or command." It refers to a government of and by a few exceedingly rich people or families who con-trol the major institutions of society and therefore have power over other people's lives. Oligarchs may try to hide their power behind those institutions, or justify their power with platitudes about the public good, or excuse their power through philanthropy and "corporate social responsibility." But no one should be fooled. Oligarchs wield power for their own benefit.

Even a system that calls itself a democracy can become an oligarchy if power becomes concentrated in the hands of a corporate and financial elite. Their power and wealth increase over time as they make laws that favor themselves, manipulate financial markets to their advantage, and create or exploit economic monopolies that put even more wealth into their own pockets.

Modern-day Russia is an oligarchy. A handful of billionaires there control most major industries and dominate politics and the economy.

America has experienced oligarchy twice before. Many of the men who founded America were slaveholding white oligarchs. The nation did not have much of a middle class. Most whites were farmers, indentured servants, farmhands, traders, day laborers, and artisans. A fifth of the population was black, almost all of them slaves.

A century later a new oligarchy emerged, comprised of men who amassed fortunes through their railroad, steel, oil, and financial empires—men such as J. Pierpont Morgan, John D. Rockefeller, Andrew Carnegie, Cornelius Vanderbilt, and Andrew Mellon. They ushered the nation into an industrial revolution that vastly expanded economic output. But they also corrupted government, brutally suppressed wages, generated unprecedented levels of inequality and urban poverty, shut down competitors, and made out like bandits—which is how they earned the sobriquet "robber barons."

World War I and the Great Depression of the 1930s eroded most of the robber barons' wealth, and with the elections of Franklin D. Roosevelt in 1932 and Democratic majorities in the House and Senate, their power was curtailed. For the next half century the gains from growth were more widely shared, and democracy became more responsive to the needs and aspirations of average Americans. During these years America created the largest middle class the world had ever seen. There was still much to do—civil rights and voting rights for African Americans, wider economic opportunities for them and for women and Latinos, protection of the environment. Yet by almost every measure the nation was making progress.

Starting around 1980, a third American oligarchy emerged. Between 1980 and 2019, the share of the nation's total household income going to the richest 1 percent more than doubled, while the earnings of the bottom 90 percent barely rose (all adjusted for inflation). CEO pay increased 940 percent, but the typical worker's pay increased 12 percent. In the 1960s, the typical CEO of a large American company earned about twenty times as much as the typical worker; by 2019, the CEO earned three hundred times as much.

Wealth inequality has exploded even faster. According to research by economists Emmanuel Saez and Gabriel Zucman, the share of total wealth held by the richest 0.1 percent—about 160,000 American households—went from less than 10 percent to 20 percent over the last four decades. They now own almost as much wealth as the bottom 90 percent of households combined. The entire bottom half of America now owns just 1.3 percent.

The only other country with similarly high levels of wealth concentration is Russia.

All this has been accompanied by a dramatic increase in the political power of the super-wealthy and an equally dramatic decline in the political influence of everyone else. As I will show, the average American now has no effect on public policy. Big corporations, CEOs, and a handful of extremely rich people have more influence than any comparable group since the robber barons. Unlike income or wealth, power is a zero-sum game. The more of it there is at the top, the less there is anywhere else.

This power shift is related to a tsunami of big money into politics. In the election cycle of 2016, the richest one-*hundredth* of 1 percent of Americans—24,949 extraordinarily wealthy people—accounted for a record-breaking 40 percent of all campaign contributions. By contrast, in 1980, the top 0.01 percent accounted for only 15 percent of all contributions.

In that same 2016 election cycle, corporations flooded the presidential, Senate, and House elections with $3.4 billion of donations. By contrast, labor unions contributed $213 million. Corporate lobbying has soared. The voices of average people have been drowned out. Meanwhile, and largely because of this vast power shift, taxes on the wealthy and on corporations have been slashed. Safety nets for the poor and middle class have begun to unravel. Public investments in education and infrastructure have waned. The "free market" has been taken over by crony capitalism, corporate bailouts, and corporate welfare.

The American oligarchy is back, with a vengeance.

．　　　．　　　．

Not all wealthy people are culpable, of course. I am not advocating class warfare. The abuse has occurred at the nexus of wealth and power, where those with great wealth use it to gain power and then utilize that power to accumulate more wealth. This is how oligarchy destroys democracy. As oligarchs fill the coffers of political candidates and deploy platoons of lobbyists and public relations flaks, they buy off democracy. Oligarchs know that politicians won't bite the hands that feed them. There will be no meaningful response to the failure of most people's paychecks to rise, nor to climate change, racism, or the soaring costs of health insurance, pharmaceuticals, college, and housing, because those are not the main concerns of the oligarchy.

As long as they control the purse strings, the oligarchs know there will be no substantial tax increases for them. Instead, their taxes will fall. There will be no antitrust enforcement to puncture the power of their giant corporations. Instead, their corporations will grow larger. There will be no meaningful constraint on Wall Street's dangerous gambling addiction. The gambling will grow. There will be no limits to CEO pay, and Wall Street hedge fund and private equity managers will rake in billions of dollars more. Government will provide even more corporate subsidies, bailouts, and loan guarantees. It will continue to eliminate protections for consumers, workers, and the environment. It will become a government for, of, and by the oligarchy.

The biggest political divide in America today is not between Republicans and Democrats. It's between democracy and oligarchy. Hearing and using the same old labels prevents most people from noticing they're being shafted.

The propagandists and demagogues who protect the oligarchy (Donald Trump included) are pouring salt into the nation's oldest wounds. They're stoking racial resentments, describing human beings as illegal aliens, fueling hatred of immigrants, and spreading fears of communists and socialists. This strategy gives the oligarchy freer rein: It distracts Americans from how the oligarchy is looting the nation, buying off politicians, and silencing critics.

The way to overcome oligarchy is for the rest of us to join together and win America back. This will require a multiracial, multiethnic coalition of working-class, poor, and middle-class Americans fighting for democracy and against concentrated power and privilege, determined to rid politics of big money, end corporate welfare and crony capitalism, bust up monopolies, stop voter suppression, and strengthen the countervailing power of labor unions, employee-owned corporations, worker cooperatives, state and local banks, and grassroots politics.

This agenda is neither right nor left. It is the bedrock for everything else America must do.

Jamie Dimon is one of the highest-paid banking and finance CEOs in the world. His 2018 compensation package was $31 million. His reported net worth is $1.6 billion. He believes he deserves every penny. "This wealthy New Yorker actually earned his money," Dimon said, comparing himself to Donald Trump. "It wasn't a gift from Daddy."

Not exactly. Dimon was born March 13, 1956, in New York, the grandson of a Greek immigrant who rose from bank clerk to stockbroker, and the son of an even more successful stockbroker. Dimon's father worked for Sanford I. Weill when Weill was already becoming the legendary head of a brokerage empire. As Weill's fortune grew, so did Dimon's father's. The family moved from Queens to an apartment on Park Avenue on Manhattan's exclusive Upper East Side. Dimon's father introduced Weill to young Jamie.

Dimon attended Browning, a New York City private school, and then Tufts University, where he majored in economics and psychology. After graduating and doing a short stint in management consulting, he got an MBA from Harvard Business School, whereupon Weill offered him a job, promising Dimon he'd have "fun" as Weill's assistant at American Express. "Jamie didn't have that sort of early struggle that most of us mere mortals have," one former colleague noted.

Dimon proved himself to be enormously talented, energetic, and able. After Weill lost a power struggle and left American Express, Dimon departed with him. Together with some other former American Express executives, they bought Commercial Credit, an underperforming consumer-lending business in Baltimore, and turned it around. Over the next decade Weill pulled off a series of audacious acquisitions culminating in the takeover of Citicorp. Under Weill's tutelage, Dimon managed financial operations at Primerica, Smith Barney, and Salomon Brothers, gaining experience and clout as he moved upward.

In 1999, Dimon couldn't move any higher at Citicorp because Weill wasn't ready to give up the reins. So Dimon moved to Chicago to take the lead at Bank One, doubling its value in four years. In 2004 he persuaded the CEO of JPMorgan Chase to purchase Bank One for $58 billion and make Dimon JPMorgan's president and chief operating officer. The next year Dimon became its CEO. The following year, he consolidated power by becoming chair of the board as well.

By 2019 JPMorgan Chase was a colossus: America's biggest credit card company, the third-ranking mortgage issuer, the biggest issuer of auto loans, one of the nation's two top investment banks. It lends and invests all over the world, every day moving more than a trillion dollars in cash and securities. Its wealth managers advise clients on where and how to invest, its analysts advise CEOs about how to boost profits, its traders move billions of dollars in pension funds and mutual funds, its investment bankers bet on movements in the values of stocks and organize initial public offerings of stock, and its managers issue mountains of credit cards and collect vast fees. In 2018 the bank controlled nearly $25 trillion worth of assets. Its own assets totaled $2.6 trillion. Its market value was over $360 billion. Its net income was $30.7 billion.

These amounts are almost impossible to comprehend. Money is the lifeblood of the system, JPMorgan is at the system's heart, and Dimon is the person in charge of keeping the heart beating healthily.

He can move vast amounts of money faster than any other person on the planet. The investor Warren Buffett, who owns shares in JPMorgan, says that when Buffett's firm, Berkshire

Hathaway, bought the Burlington Northern Railroad for $26 billion in the fall of 2009, he called Dimon on the Tuesday just before the announcement of the deal and said, "Jamie, I need $8 billion!" "You got it," Buffett says Dimon told him. Buffett adds, "Even with some of the other big banks, that's not something you could do on the phone."

Dimon has also built a formidable lobbying machine in Washington—far larger than the lobbying machines of Wall Street's other big banks—replete with politically connected former congressional staffers who battle daily on behalf of JPMorgan in the halls of Congress, administrative agencies, and the courts. JPMorgan also keeps on hand a fleet of Washington lawyers, tax attorneys, political consultants, and public relations professionals.

In 2017 Dimon became chair of the Business Roundtable, an association of 192 CEOs of America's biggest companies, with an outsized voice in Washington. In 2019 the Business Roundtable's board of directors included Mary Barra, chairman and CEO of General Motors; Gregory Hayes, chair and CEO of United Technologies; Alex Gorsky, chair and CEO of Johnson & Johnson; Lynn Good, chair and CEO of Duke Energy; Douglas McMillon, president and CEO of Walmart; Dennis Muilenburg, chair and CEO of Boeing; Chuck Robbins, chair and CEO of Cisco Systems; Virginia Rometty, chair and CEO of IBM; Arne Sorenson, president and CEO of Marriott; Randall Stephenson, chair and CEO of AT&T; Douglas Peterson, president and CEO of S&P Global; Larry Merlo, president and CEO of CVS Health; and Marilyn Hewson, chair and CEO of Lockheed Martin.

As a lifelong Democrat, Dimon is a friend of Bill Clinton. He supported Obama in 2008 and mentored people who became high officials in the Obama White House. At Obama's inauguration in 2009, Dimon said to the incoming president, "Tell me what you need. I'll send people down here. I'll do anything." In 2009, *The New York Times* called Dimon "Obama's favorite banker." Dimon supported Hillary Clinton in 2016, but he can be a switch-hitter. He is on good terms with Republican leaders.

Jamie Dimon comes as close as anyone to embodying the American system as it functions today. He's a member in good standing of the American oligarchy. If you want to understand that oligarchy, you need to understand Dimon.

CHAPTER 2

Patriot First?

JAMIE DIMON frankly acknowledges the dysfunctions of the system. In his yearly letters to JPMorgan's shareholders and in his numerous public appearances, he publicly laments many of our major problems.

In his 2019 letter he conceded that "a big chunk of [Americans] have been left behind" and that "forty percent of Americans make less than $15 an hour, 40% . . . can't afford a $400 bill, whether it's medical or fixing their car; 15% of Americans make minimum wages, 70,000 die from opioids."

In 2018 he told JPMorgan's shareholders that "middle class incomes have been stagnant for years. Income inequality has gotten worse. . . . More than 28 million Americans don't have medical insurance at all. And, surprisingly, 25% of those eligible for various types of federal assistance programs don't get any help." He cautioned that "no one can claim that the promise of equal opportunity is being offered to all Americans through our education systems, nor are those who have run afoul of our justice system getting the second chance that many of them deserve. And we have been debating immigration reform for 30 years. Simply put, the social needs of far too many of our citizens are not being met."

In his 2017 letter he warned, "We should be ringing the national alarm bell that inner city schools are failing our children," and noted that "over the last 16 years, we have spent trillions of dollars on wars when we could have been investing that money productively."

He told bankers at a financial conference that "I want to help lower-wage people more than I want to help you." He opined on CNN that the U.S. economy is "fundamentally anti-poor." He charged that "if you live in certain parts of town, if you're white or Hispanic or black, you can pretty much be left behind." He told the Economic Club of Chicago that racial discrimination isn't adequately understood by whites. "If you're white, paint yourself black and walk down the street one day, and you'll probably have a little more empathy for how some of these folks get treated," and he called for making "a special effort because this is a special problem."

His liberalism extends to other hot-button issues. In 2017 Dimon told CNBC that he opposed Trump's plan to pull the United States out of the Paris Agreement on Climate Change. After the August 2019 mass shootings in El Paso, Texas, and Dayton, Ohio, Dimon wrote a well-publicized email to his employees calling on them to "recommit ourselves to work for a more equitable, just and safe society."

Yet for all his liberal outspokenness, Dimon never mentions America's growing concentration of wealth and power, and the tight connection between the two. He doesn't talk about the role of big money in persuading the public they should vote for particular candidates or against others, support or oppose specific legislation, be concerned about this problem or that, or believe one set of facts or another. He doesn't mention how wealth buys access to politicians and sometimes even their votes, or how the prospect of lucrative jobs on Wall Street upon retirement might tempt some public officials to pull their punches.

Still, credit Dimon for putting his (or, more accurately, JPMorgan's) money where his mouth is. Dimon takes seriously the idea that corporations like JPMorgan have social responsibilities. "Most people consider corporate responsibility to be enhanced philanthropy [but it] is far more than just that," he has said. "We finance more than $2 billion in affordable housing each year; we do extensive lending in low- and moderate-income neighborhoods; we lend to and finance small businesses around the country; and we design products and services in financial education for lower income individuals."

In 2019 he announced a five-year, $350 million program to help train workers for the jobs of the future. A big chunk of that sum would be targeted to helping poor young people, including those who have been stigmatized by criminal records, making it hard for them to find work. "Kids aren't getting the education they need to get a job," Dimon said. "And I'm talking about a real job."

In 2018 JPMorgan Chase announced a $500 million AdvancingCities initiative to invest in struggling American metropolises. It was an expansion of a plan begun in 2013 to invest over $100 million in Detroit after the city declared bankruptcy. The bank has made low-cost loans, renovated affordable housing, and put money into workforce training.

These are noble efforts, but they're tiny relative to the size of the problem they're meant to address. They are also small relative to JPMorgan's net income, which in 2018 was roughly one hundred times the size of its worker-training program. I should also point out that its $30.7 billion net income that year was more than a third higher than its net income the previous year. About half of the gain between 2017 and 2018 came from savings from the giant corporate tax cut enacted at the end of 2017, which reduced corporate taxes from 35 percent of corporate income to 21 percent.

Dimon lobbied Congress personally and intensively for the tax cut, and he got the Business Roundtable to join him. Overall, the tax cut increased the federal debt by $1.9 trillion while delivering no measurable benefits to America's working class or poor, and almost nothing trickled down. Corporations used most of the tax savings to buy back their shares of stock, generating a short-lived sugar high for the stock market. The vastly enlarged federal debt will surely reduce what the federal government can spend on education and affordable housing in struggling American cities. In other words, although Dimon deserves credit for being the only Wall Street executive with the vision and fortitude to initiate a number of programs for the poor, subtract his success in getting the tax cut and America's poor are indubitably worse off.

A few hundred million dollars for struggling cities and workforce training is also chicken feed compared to Wall Street's yearly bonus pool, which in 2018 came to $27.5 billion. That sum, not incidentally, is more than three times the combined incomes of the approximately 600,000 Americans employed full-time at the minimum wage—some of whom work in Detroit and other struggling American cities. Yet Dimon has not suggested raising the minimum wage. In fact, the Business Roundtable has lobbied against any increase in the federal minimum wage, which was last raised in 2009 to $7.25 per hour. Some JPMorgan tellers don't earn nearly enough to make ends meet.

But a few hundred million dollars is certainly a good investment in public relations, especially for a big Wall Street bank that, together with other Wall Street banks, brought the economy to the brink of collapse in 2008 and caused millions of people to lose their jobs, homes, and savings.

In recent years, "corporate social responsibility," as it is termed, has become the supposed answer to the failings of capitalism. It's a hot topic in business schools. Hundreds of corporate conferences are held on it annually. Tens of thousands of executives listen attentively to consultants who explain its importance. The world's top CEOs, gathering annually at the World Economic Forum in Davos, Switzerland, solemnly proclaim their commitment to it. Former president Bill Clinton had a global initiative based on it. Companies routinely produce glossy reports touting their dedication to it. At least eight hundred mutual funds worldwide are devoted to it. The United Nations Global Compact, launched at Davos in 1999, enumerates goals for it. Great Britain has a minister for it.

Most of this is in earnest, much is sincere, and some of it has had a positive impact. But all of it has occurred outside of the democratic process. None of it has reallocated power in the system or changed the rules of the game. To view corporate social responsibility as a new form of capitalism diverts attention from the far more difficult and important task of strengthening democracy and thwarting oligarchy.

In fact, the upsurge of interest in corporate social responsibility is directly related to decreasing confidence in democracy, precisely because big money has overwhelmed it. "Government is failing to provide leadership on environmental concerns, and industry has grown more willing to address them," says Jonathan Lash, former president of the World Resources Institute. But don't be fooled. Government is failing to address such issues because big corporations have become so effective at preventing government from addressing them.

It's easy to understand why big businesses like JPMorgan have embraced corporate social responsibility with such verve. The soothing promise of responsibility can forestall laws and regulations that require it. As the theologian Reinhold Niebuhr observed, "The powerful are more inclined to be generous than to grant social justice." Commitments to social responsibility are also conveniently reassuring to talented or privileged young people who want to do good while also doing well, and who don't want to acknowledge the cruel joke that, as Anand Giridharadas, author of *Winners Take All,* has pointed out, people with the most to lose from genuine social change have put themselves in charge of social change. Dimon is correct that a big chunk of Americans have been left behind, but he ignores the role he and his bank have played in leaving them. JPMorgan paid $13 billion to settle Justice Department claims that it defrauded borrowers and investors in the years leading up to the 2008 financial crisis, when he was at the helm. Among its victims were many left-behind Americans.

When Dimon ran Chicago's Bank One, he was ruthless about maximizing credit card fees. "Yes, he is a man of the people because he wants a hand in every wallet," Janet Tavakoli, a derivatives consultant, told Reuters. "His game is to get as many fees as possible." On his watch, Bank One's credit card unit settled a three-year investigation into alleged deceptive marketing practices and paid a $1.3 million fine to state attorneys general.

In June 2019, JPMorgan reintroduced forced arbitration in credit card disputes, requiring that customers submit to closed-door hearings with an arbitrator picked by JPMorgan rather than have access to a court of law or band together in class-action lawsuits. Forced arbitration tilts the game in favor of the bank and leaves more Americans behind. A study conducted at Stanford University by professors Mark Egan, Gregor Matvos, and Amit Seru that analyzed more than nine thousand arbitration cases found that companies often pick arbiters who have track records of deciding in favor of the business.

Contract disputes are an expected feature of capitalism, of course, but how they're resolved is very much a question of power. Wall Street banks have repeatedly beaten back bills to stop mandatory arbitration. In this age of oligarchy, no one should be surprised at this except those who stubbornly cling to the fiction of a free market divorced from politics and power.

So, too, with the environment. Climate change already is having a devastating impact around the world—including on left-behind Americans who can't afford homes able to withstand storms and floods and who have no insurance against climate catastrophe. Although Dimon publicly opposed Trump's plan to pull the United States out of the Paris Agreement, between 2016 and 2018 JPMorgan invested nearly $196 billion in oil and gas, which was nearly a third more than the next biggest bank investor in fossil fuels. JPMorgan is also among the biggest backers of fracking. It is the major bank lender and investor in companies active in the Permian Basin, the epicenter of the climate-threatening surge of oil and gas production. It has provided the most financing to liquefied natural gas projects, Arctic oil and gas projects, and ultra-deep-water oil and gas extraction. A 2019 report issued by a coalition of six major environmental groups named Dimon the "world's worst banker of climate change." The likely consequence: More Americans are left behind.

Dimon decries discrimination and points to the money JPMorgan is investing in poor cities. But he ignores the bank's role in preventing poor African Americans from getting loans. In January 2017 JPMorgan agreed to pay $55 million to settle a Justice Department lawsuit accusing it of discriminating against minority borrowers by allowing its mortgage brokers to charge them higher interest on home loans than it charged white borrowers with the same credit profile, causing the black

borrowers to pay tens of millions of dollars in additional mortgage costs. According to the Justice Department's complaint,
an African American taking out a $191,100 loan paid on aver-
age $1,126 more over the first five years of the loan than a white
borrower. A Latino borrower with a $236,800 loan paid on
average $968 more than a non-Latino white borrower. JPMor-
gan didn't require mortgage brokers to document the reasons
for changing rates, it failed to address racial discrimination,
and even encouraged the discrimination to continue. The
result: More Americans are left behind.

Dimon publicly frets about other social problems that disproportionately affect lower-income Americans, such as the
easy availability of guns. But he doesn't acknowledge JPMorgan's role as the largest bank in the United States providing
financial services to gun makers and gun retailers and loans to
gun buyers. If Dimon were serious about controlling the use of
guns, he could stop this financing and urge other banks to do
the same. He could have his banking and credit card systems
track gun sales. He could use his formidable lobbying prowess,
and that of the Business Roundtable, to enact laws requiring
that financial institutions create a world-class system for track-
ing gun sales with built-in safeguards.

But he has not. The result: More Americans are killed,
injured, and left behind.

Dimon expresses concern about workers who don't earn
enough to live on, but, as I said, JPMorgan pays its bank tellers
very little. In April 2019, at a hearing of the House Financial
Services Committee, Representative Katie Porter noted that
the starting salary for a JPMorgan bank teller in her district

in Irvine, California, was $24,000, which left the teller $567 a month short of what she needed to live on. "How should she manage this budget shortfall while she's working full-time at your bank?" Porter asked Dimon.

"I don't know, I'd have to think about that," Dimon said.

"Would you recommend that she take out a JPMorgan Chase credit card and run a deficit?" Porter continued.

"I don't know, I'd have to think about it," Dimon repeated.

"Would you recommend that she overdraft at your bank and be charged overdraft fees?" Porter asked.

"I don't know, I'd have to think about it."

"Mr. Dimon, you know how to spend $31 million in salary, and you can't figure out how to make up a $567 shortfall?"

After Bank of America agreed to increase its minimum wage to $20 an hour by 2021, Dimon was asked if JPMorgan would match it. "It's not an arms race," he said.

How does one square the public Jamie Dimon with the Jamie Dimon who's chair and CEO of JPMorgan Chase? He says he's a patriot before he's a CEO, but in all the ways I've noted, he behaves as if his first responsibility is to maximize JPMorgan's profits.

The underlying issue here isn't hypocrisy. The world is filled with people who say one thing and do another. And let's be clear: JPMorgan expects Dimon's first priority to be JPMorgan's profitability. That's his job and he's paid handsomely for it. The underlying problem is power and deception. Dimon has enormous public and political influence. When he takes public stands on issues—when he announces his support for Trump's tax cut and lobbies Congress intensely for it, or comes out against Representative Alexandria Ocasio-Cortez's and Senator Edward Markey's Green New Deal, or publicly opposes Senator Elizabeth Warren's wealth tax, or proffers his alleged economic expertise on CNBC and other media outlets, or urges members of Congress to loosen bank regulations, or warns Democrats against nominating someone who is not viewed as a political moderate—he clothes himself in the garb of the public interest. He poses as a public leader whose primary interest is the good of the nation rather than the good of JPMorgan.

But he harbors a profound conflict of interest because his job is to do whatever he can to boost the profits of JPMorgan, even if and when that goal conflicts with the public interest. And one of the ways he achieves that goal is to exercise significant influence over government. So how can the public, the media, and members of Congress ever trust his advice on the economy, taxes, financial regulation, the environment, widening inequality, or anything else? How can we believe that his initiatives on corporate social responsibility are anything other than public relations? Why should we think that he and his Business Roundtable seek any goal other than making more money for themselves and their firms?

The Business Roundtable's motto—"More than Leaders. Leadership"—suggests a purpose higher than making its member companies richer. When Dimon became chair of the

Roundtable, he promised that by "working together" government and business would "build on pro-growth economic policies," and that these would be good for everyone. "Do I want everyone to have access to health care? Yes. Do I want inner-city kids to graduate from schools? Yes. Personally, I don't mind paying higher taxes," Dimon said. "But don't mess up the machine that creates the value so you can do these things. The economy is what gave us everything."

Yet when the Roundtable lobbied for the Trump tax cut, it publicly asserted that it "will put America on a path of accelerated economic growth" and that "the U.S. tax system has become an anti-competitive drag on the U.S. economy." In truth, the last four decades have revealed an almost total disconnect between the growth and competitiveness of large American corporations and the well-being of most Americans. Most of the benefits of growth and competitiveness have been captured by those at the top. Growth has also generated more carbon in the atmosphere and more plastic in the oceans, making humankind worse off.

In August 2019 the Business Roundtable issued a highly publicized statement expressing "a fundamental commitment to *all* of our stakeholders" (emphasis in original), including a commitment to compensating all its employees "fairly," as well as "supporting the communities in which we work," and protecting the environment "by embracing sustainable practices across our businesses." The statement—signed by 181 CEOs of major American corporations—concluded that "each of our stakeholders is essential" and committed "to deliver value to all of them."

But it seems dubious that JPMorgan and the other 180 big corporations whose CEOs signed this pledge are prepared to sacrifice share values (as well as all the executive pay tied to those shares) in order to raise worker pay, achieve greater diversity, remain in communities even when somewhere else on the globe becomes a cheaper place to do business, and better protect the environment. As evidenced by their relentless lobbying for the large corporate tax cut, they are not prepared to raise taxes on themselves and their corporations to pay for needed services in their communities. Twenty-one of the corporations whose CEOs signed the statement paid no federal income taxes in 2018, courtesy of those lobbying efforts. One of the signers was Jeff Bezos, the multi-billionaire CEO of Amazon and of its Whole Foods subsidiary. Just weeks after the statement appeared, Whole Foods announced it would be cutting medical benefits for its entire part-time workforce—at a total annual savings of what Bezos himself made in two hours.

If the Business Roundtable CEOs were serious about being committed to all their stakeholders, they'd seek legislation that would bind them and every other major corporation to those commitments—legislation, for example, requiring worker representatives on their boards, mandating that workers receive a certain percentage of shares of stock, requiring large companies to provide medical benefits even for part-time workers, forcing corporations to recognize a union when a majority of workers want one, and giving communities where they operate a say on whether corporations that have been their mainstays should be able to abandon them.

More likely, the CEOs signed this statement in order to ward off this sort of legislation. In reality, the CEOs of the Business Roundtable no longer provide good jobs to a broad swath of Americans. For forty years they have fought unions mercilessly, outsourced jobs abroad, loaded up on labor-replacing technologies without retraining their workers, abandoned their communities when they could do things more cheaply elsewhere, and used their political clout to cut their own taxes, roll back regulatory protections, and oppose legislation that would provide kids with better schools and give everyone better access to health care.

The "machine" of the American economy, as Dimon calls it, has not been working for most Americans. It is creating value only for a precious few. By "working together," government and business have rigged the game. By now, most Americans are aware of that rigging. But nothing is stopping Dimon and other major CEOs from putting an end to it. They could use their formidable political clout to reduce the need for candidates to raise funds from corporations and wealthy individuals by supporting public financing for campaigns backed by small donors. They could push for stricter limits on the "revolving door" between industry and government, and laws requiring full disclosure of the sources of all campaign funding. They could seek a constitutional amendment limiting lobbying and campaign spending.

Rather than announce token jobs programs, spreading some money around poor cities, lobbying for lower corporate taxes and fewer regulations whose benefits don't trickle down, and putting out nice statements about corporate responsibility, these top CEOs could seek to increase the economic and political power of all Americans—giving them a greater voice at their workplace, in their communities, and in Washington, so they won't need corporate philanthropy.

Nothing is stopping them except their own parched, self-serving notion of leadership as maximizing profits and share-holder value. Yet as heads of institutions with the greatest influence over American politics, don't they also have a duty to the common good? They should be using their unrivaled influence to push for a society where no corporation or set of people can ever again become as rich and powerful as they are. After all, what does leadership really mean? What's the value of all the reassuring public statements by Dimon and the Business Roundtable? For forty years the CEOs of America's largest corporations and Wall Street banks have abdicated their responsibility to America. We are now living with the consequences of that abdication. Dimon and the Business Round-table can see them as well as anyone.

I'm sure Dimon and the other members of the Business Roundtable consider themselves patriots. But they are not patriots first. They are CEOs first. And as the system is now organized, their goal must be to make as much money as possible. Shareholders expect no less. If investors wanted to be philanthropic they would put their money into a charity.

Reform of our common life will not be led by socially responsible corporations or by enlightened CEOs. It will be led by concerned and active citizens.

·　　·　　·

Jamie Dimon is not the only member of America's oligarchy to acknowledge what has happened without admitting his own complicity. Over and over, we have heard apocalyptic prophecies by oligarchs unwilling to sacrifice any of their own wealth and power to prevent an apocalypse. Consider Ray Dalio, founder of Bridgewater Associates, the largest hedge fund in the world, with $160 billion in assets under management. Dalio's personal net worth, as of April 2019, was estimated to be $18 billion.

In early 2019 Dalio issued a five-thousand-word treatise entitled "Why and How Capitalism Needs to be Reformed (Part 1)," in which he concluded that the system "is not working well for the majority of Americans because it's producing self-reinforcing spirals up for the haves and down for the have-nots." The widening income and wealth gaps are "bringing about damaging domestic and international conflicts and weakening America's condition." Dalio foresees one of two outcomes: Either we "re-engineer the system so that the pie is both divided and grown well" or else "we will have great conflict and some form of revolution that will hurt most everyone and will shrink the pie."

Dalio proposes the system be reengineered not by stopping hedge funds and other big investors like him from forcing companies to squeeze out every ounce of profits, typically by pushing down wages and by abandoning workers and communities; not by changing corporate governance to give workers more say or giving them more ownership of the companies they work in; not by busting up giant Wall Street hedge funds and banks—not, in short, by doing anything that could possibly threaten Dalio's own considerable wealth and power. Instead, he suggests convening a "bipartisan commission." Hello?

Several billionaires entered the 2020 presidential race. One of them, Tom Steyer, whose net worth as of 2019 was $1.6 billion, made "fighting inequality" a priority. To his credit, Steyer saw the connection between vast wealth and government corruption. "We have to break the corporate stranglehold on our democracy," he said. "The system is broken."

But wait. Steyer made his fortune as the founder of Farallon Capital, a hedge fund that invested in coal mines, coal-fired plants, and private prisons. He planned to finance his own presidential race by spending $100 million of his own money on it, which just about equaled the interest he earned from his assets in 2018. In just the first six weeks of his campaign, he doled out $12 million on digital and television ads, more than any other Democratic presidential candidate had spent in six months. The ads pounded away at how "our democracy has been purchased," but nowhere did Steyer propose a law preventing billionaires like him from purchasing an election.

Billionaire Michael Bloomberg also sought to purchase the presidency in 2020. His $57 billion fortune made him the ninth richest person in America and fourteenth richest in the world. Bloomberg saw nothing wrong with the oligarchy's takeover of the American system. In the 2018 midterm elections, he spent more than $110 million boosting Democratic candidates. His wealth would allow him to self-finance his own presidential campaign. "Democrats shouldn't be embarrassed about our system," he argued, warning that a wealth tax was "probably unconstitutional" and could wreck the economy.

Then there was Howard Schultz, founder and CEO of Starbucks. Shortly after Schultz announced his possible interest in the presidency, CNN gave him an hour-long town hall in which he fielded questions from an audience. Not everyone who expresses a possible interest in being president merits a CNN town hall, but Schultz got one because he is worth over $3.6 billion. Someone with that much money can buy so much advertising and self-promotion that he automatically becomes a serious presidential candidate just by virtue of having the capacity to self-finance his presidential campaign. Months later, having received almost no public support for his candidacy, Schultz dropped out of the race, saying he would use the money he was prepared to commit to his presidential campaign "to transform our broken system," promote "civility," and "help address widening inequality" instead. It never seemed to occur to Schultz that the breakage, incivility, and inequality might be related to people earning coffee grounds while those at the top run off with the Super Venti Flat White. In 2018, Starbucks paid its baristas an average of $11 an hour, while Schultz's compensation was $30.2 million.

Schultz has touted Starbucks' social responsibility, such as the bracelets it sells for $5 whose proceeds it donates to support investment in poor communities. Yet at the same time, Starbucks has kept some $1.9 billion offshore to avoid paying U.S. taxes, meaning hundreds of millions in lost tax revenues that might otherwise have helped poor communities. Social responsibility, my macchiato.

·　　·　　·

Dimon, Dalio, Steyer, Bloomberg, and Schultz all say they care about America and worry that the system is breaking down. But they are among the biggest beneficiaries of how the system is now organized. It is folly to think that any of them would lead the charge to change it.

CHAPTER 3

Socialism for the Rich,
Harsh Capitalism for the Rest

JAMIE DIMON is among the most influential Democrats on Wall Street, so his opinions carry particular weight in Democratic circles. In April 2019 he warned against the direction some congressional Democrats and presidential candidates were taking the party, writing in his annual shareholder letter that it amounted to socialism. "Socialism inevitably produces stagnation, corruption and often worse—such as authoritarian government officials who often have an increasing ability to interfere with both the economy and individual lives—which they frequently do to maintain power," he wrote, adding that socialism would be "a disaster for our country."

It's not clear exactly what Dimon means by socialism. "Socialism" was the scare word used by the oligarchy of the Gilded Age when America began to regulate and break up their giant corporations. It was the term used by the American

Liberty League in 1935 to attack President Franklin D. Roosevelt's proposal for Social Security. "Socialism is the epithet they have hurled at every advance the people have made," President Harry Truman observed. It was "what they called public power . . . bank deposit insurance . . . free and independent labor organizations . . . anything that helps all the people." Every time over the last century Americans have sought to pool their resources for the common good, the wealthy and powerful have used the bogeyman of "socialism" to try to stop them.

If by "socialism" Dimon meant social insurance, the brute fact is that by 2019 America spent very little on safety nets compared to other advanced nations. Almost 30 million Americans still lack health insurance, most workers who lose their job aren't eligible for unemployment insurance, one out of five American children lives in poverty, and nearly 51 million households can't afford basic monthly expenses such as housing, food, child care, and transportation. Our infrastructure is literally crumbling, our classrooms are overcrowded, and our teachers are paid far less than workers in the private sector with comparable levels of education.

But America *does* practice one form of socialism— socialism for the rich. Exhibit A is the bailout of Wall Street in 2008. Dimon was at the helm when JPMorgan received $25 billion from the federal government to help stem the financial crisis, which had been brought on largely by the careless and fraudulent lending practices of JPMorgan and other big banks. Dimon himself was paid $20 million that year. If this isn't socialism, what is? In the wake of that crisis, 8.7 million people lost their jobs, sending the unemployment rate soaring to 10 percent in 2008. Total U.S. household net worth dropped by $11.1 trillion. Housing prices dropped by one-third nation-wide from their 2006 peak, ultimately causing some 10 million people to lose their homes.

In March 2009 President Obama summoned Dimon and other top executives to the White House and warned them, "My administration is the only thing between you and the pitchforks." But Obama never publicly rebuked Dimon or the other big bankers. When asked about the generous pay Dimon and other Wall Street CEOs continued to rake in, Obama defended them as "very savvy businessmen" and said he didn't "begrudge peoples' success or wealth. That's part of the free market system." What free market system? Taxpayers had just bailed out the banks, and the bank CEOs were still taking in fat paychecks. Rather than defend those paychecks, Obama might have demanded that the Wall Street banks help under-water homeowners on Main Street as a condition of getting bailed out.

JPMorgan returned its bailout money quicker than other big banks, but it has continued to make a nice profit from being "too big to fail." By 2019, America's five biggest banks, including Dimon's, accounted for 46 percent of all U.S. bank depos-its. In the early 1990s, they had accounted for only 12 percent. Their giant size has translated into a huge but hidden federal subsidy estimated to be $83 billion annually, reflecting the pre-mium investors are willing to pay for the stocks and bonds of banks they believe are too big to fail.

Dimon says it's wrong to "vilify" people who succeed under

free market capitalism, like himself. But he has an odd view of free market capitalism. It seems not to include the bank bailout and its ongoing $83 billion hidden government insurance. Take this subsidy away and Wall Street's entire bonus pool would disappear, along with most of its profits, and Dimon would be worth far less than $1.6 billion.

A few years after the crisis Dimon told Roger Lowenstein of *The New York Times* that "no bank should be too big to fail" and that if JPMorgan couldn't pay its bills, "Morgan should have to file for bankruptcy." Dimon was either stunningly naïve or was pandering to *Times* readers, saying what he assumed they wanted to hear. Given the mammoth size and dominance of JPMorgan and the other behemoths on the Street, their failures would put the national economy into a tailspin. Bankruptcy is out of the question. Dimon knew this better than anyone.

By 2018, a full decade after the crisis, the American economy had regained all the jobs it had lost and more, and housing prices had rebounded. But many of the deepest wounds had still not healed. Median household income, adjusted for inflation, had barely budged over the decade, although the incomes of the wealthiest had soared. Median household wealth (mostly contained in the value of people's homes) was $97,000, still far below what it had been in 2007 ($126,000). Almost a third of adult millennials still lived at home. The crisis stunted the economy so much that every man, woman, and child in America lost the equivalent of $70,000 compared to what they would have earned had the Great Recession never happened, according to calculations by the Federal Reserve Bank of San Francisco.

The economy was saved, but many things could have been done to lessen the pain for average people. One sensible proposal would have let bankruptcy judges restructure shaky home mortgages, so borrowers didn't owe as much and could therefore pay their mortgage bills and remain in their homes. Borrowers can already use bankruptcy to protect their vacation homes and investment properties, so why not their primary homes? Yet the big banks, led by Dimon, opposed the proposal. They thought they'd do better by squeezing as much as they could out of distressed homeowners, and then collecting as much as they could on foreclosed homes. In April 2008, Dimon and the banks succeeded: The Senate formally voted down a bill allowing bankruptcy judges to modify mortgages on primary residences to help financially distressed homeowners.

Research shows that most people pay their bills until some unforeseen event—loss of a job, a serious medical problem, a divorce—makes doing so impossible. Absent supports typical in European countries—such as anti-layoff regulations, universal health care, and paid family leave—Americans are especially vulnerable to serious financial disruptions. Without access to bankruptcy to protect their homes, they and their families can find themselves out on the street. Here again, Jamie Dimon seems not to have considered his role in leaving Americans behind. (The 2005 bankruptcy act—another product of Wall Street lobbying—prevents graduates from seeking to have their student loan debt forgiven under bankruptcy.)

Bankruptcy is part of the free market, but, like all other aspects of the market, its rules are determined through politics, and over the last four decades Wall Street has become far more politically powerful than Main Street. That's why the biggest banks got bailed out and didn't have to use bankruptcy, while homeowners did not get bailed out and were not allowed to use bankruptcy. Recall that there is no free market separate and apart from government. Government sets the rules of the game. The issue is who has most influence over those rules. In the era of oligarchy, the rules are being set by those at the top.

To the conservative mind, socialism means getting something for doing nothing. This pretty much describes Adam Neumann, the young, charismatic billionaire founder of WeWork, an office-sharing start-up. Wanting to get into the action early with the hope of leading WeWork's initial public offering, JPMorgan poured so much money into the company and into Neumann's own pockets that Neumann reportedly described Dimon as his "personal banker." Neumann used the money to fund projects such as buildings that he leased back to WeWork, and a lifestyle that included a $60 million private jet, a sixty-acre estate in Westchester County, a residence in Manhattan's upscale Gramercy Park neighborhood, a $22 million home in the Bay Area, another in the Hamptons, in-house concerts, a personal spa attached to his office, and a Maybach luxury car. WeWork never showed a profit. In the end, it all fell apart after the bank pressed Neumann to disclose his personal conflicts of interest in WeWork's filings for the initial public offering and potential investors fled. Neumann was ousted in October 2019 and walked away with over $1 billion. Yet most other WeWork employees were subject to harsh capitalism. They were left holding nearly worthless stock options. Thousands were set to be laid off.

Getting something for nothing also describes General Motors' receipt of $600 million in federal contracts, plus $500 million in tax breaks, in the two years after Donald Trump took office. Some of this corporate welfare went into the pockets of GM executives. Chair and CEO Mary Barra raked in almost $22 million in total compensation in 2017 alone. GM employees, on the other hand, have been subject to harsh capitalism. GM announced in 2018 that it planned to lay off more than fourteen thousand workers and close three assembly plants and two component factories. In early 2019 it shut its giant plant in Lordstown, Ohio, which Trump had vowed to save. "Don't move. Don't sell your house," he had told a rally. A decade earlier, when GM was on the brink of collapse, American taxpayers rescued it with a $50 billion bailout. As part of the deal, GM workers allowed the company to make new hires at about half its prevailing hourly wage and with skimpier retirement benefits, bring on temp workers at even lower rates, and outsource more jobs abroad. Yet once GM was back to making big profits, it didn't raise wages or stop outsourcing. This led almost fifty thousand workers to go on strike in September 2019.

Under socialism for the rich, it is possible to screw up big-time and still reap generous rewards—if you're a CEO. Equifax's Richard Smith retired in 2017 with an $18 million pension in the wake of a security breach that exposed to hackers the personal information of 145 million customers. Wells Fargo's Carrie Tolstedt departed with a $125 million exit package after being in charge of the unit that opened more than 2 million unauthorized customer accounts. Boeing CEO Dennis Muilenburg raked in $23 million in 2018, up 27 percent from the year before, notwithstanding the corporation's deadly, defective 737 Max airliner. McDonald's CEO Stephen Easterbrook, fired in 2019 for having an inappropriate relationship with an employee, received a severance package of nearly $42 million—more than double the $15.9 million he made in 2018.

In 2019, OxyContin maker Purdue Pharma sought bankruptcy protection from lawsuits seeking to hold it accountable for its role in the nation's opioid epidemic. Yet in the preceding year, the company paid its CEO, Craig Landau, $9 million and board chairman, Steve Miller, nearly $4 million, and five other board members a combined $3.7 million.

In 2018, the stock market posted its worst annual performance since the financial crisis. The median shareholder return for the largest five hundred corporations was a negative 5.8 percent. But their top executives got raises of 5 percent or more, with the typical CEO pay reaching a record $12.4 million, according to an analysis by *The Wall Street Journal*. Big financial firms did even worse for their shareholders (a negative 17 percent for the year) but even better for their CEOs (median raises of 8.5 percent).

JPMorgan closed the year with a negative 6.7 percent total shareholder return, yet the bank paid Jamie Dimon $31 million, up from $28.3 million in 2017. That may have been because its profits were up, as I've noted. (There's not always a direct relationship between year-by-year profits and share prices.) Nonetheless, Institutional Shareholder Services, which advises major investors on how to vote, found Dimon's compensation to be excessive and recommended that shareholders vote against it. It didn't matter. Even if a majority of shareholders voted against Dimon's pay, the board was under no obligation to change it. Shareholder votes on executive pay are merely advisory. This is the American system. When asked by CBS's Lesley Stahl whether his pay was too high, Dimon said he had nothing to do with it" and "leave[s] it to the board to set my compensation." But Dimon is chair of the board—simultaneously JPMorgan's CEO and its board chair—and it's unlikely the board would act against its own chair. Occupying both roles is perfectly legal, but it means even less corporate oversight. This, too, is how the system has come to be organized.

The contrast between Dimon's $31 million pay and what most Americans took home drew public comment and even ridicule. After Morehouse College's commencement speaker, billionaire investor Robert Smith, promised to cover all the student debt of its graduating students, the satirical *Onion* posted an article entitled "Chase CEO Giving Commencement Pledges to Double Whole Class's Student Loan Debt," accompanied by a large photo of Dimon.

Although JPMorgan has been deep in legal hot water, those problems and consequential fines have had no effect on

Dimon's pay. In the bank's 2013 quarterly report, its list of legal imbroglios ran to nine pages of small print: improper energy trading, fraud in collecting credit card debt, misrepresenting the quality of mortgages in securities sold to investors, misleading credit card customers, bribing officials in foreign countries to buy certain securities, illegally foreclosing on mortgages, covering up Bernie Madoff's Ponzi scheme, manipulating the foreign exchange market.

That year the bank paid out more than $20 billion to settle the claims but still made a profit of $17.9 billion. So JPMorgan's board voted to boost Dimon's pay to $20 million, a 74 percent increase over the year before, which came out to about $1 million for every billion dollars JPMorgan had been fined for illegal activities. In fact, Dimon's star actually rose at the bank when, due to his personal connections, he negotiated with the government directly. He reached out to then attorney general Eric Holder to get a $13 billion settlement on claims of mortgage fraud. A few months later, he personally approached Preet Bharara, the United States attorney in Manhattan who had led the investigation into the Madoff Ponzi scheme, and settled that one, too. Still, JPMorgan's board struggled to strike the right balance in determining Dimon's compensation, according to the people briefed on the matter. Cutting his pay would have sent a message to bank regulators that the firm understood it had done wrong, but might have angered Dimon. In the end, the board opted to please Dimon rather than its regulators.

The decision made sense in narrow economic terms. More money was made by ignoring the laws and paying the fines than by following the laws and forgoing the business. The same logic applied to Citigroup's $7 billion settlement over similar frauds in 2014, and to Bank of America's record-shattering $16.65 billion settlement. In fact, on news of Bank of America's settlement, its stock price rose. When Holder announced the guilty plea of the giant bank Crédit Suisse to criminal charges of aiding rich Americans in avoiding paying taxes, he crowed, "This case shows that no financial institution, no matter its size or global reach, is above the law." But financial markets shrugged off Crédit Suisse's $2.8 billion fine, and the bank's shares rose the day the guilty plea was announced. Its CEO even sounded upbeat, noting that "discussions with clients have been very reassuring." That was probably because the Justice Department hadn't even required the bank to turn over its list of tax-cheating clients.

Corporations do not automatically obey laws. They weigh the size of the penalty relative to the gain from law breaking. In the age of oligarchy, laws are window dressing when penalties aren't high enough and the people responsible for the lawbreaking are not held accountable. Unless the government prosecutes individuals or at least claws back their pay, the law is not of particular concern to the inhabitants of C-suites. Eleven years after Wall Street's near meltdown, not a single major financial executive had been convicted or even indicted for crimes that wiped out the savings of countless Americans. Contrast this with a teenager who is imprisoned for years for selling an ounce of marijuana.

Socialism for the rich means the oligarchy is not held

accountable. Harsh capitalism for the many means most Americans are at risk for events over which they have no control—such as the closing of factories across the Midwest or a Wall Street financial crisis—and have no safety nets to catch them if they fall.

CHAPTER 4

The System of Corruption

ACCORDING TO A STUDY published in 2014 by Princeton professor Martin Gilens and Northwestern professor Benjamin Page, the preferences of the typical American have no influence at all on legislation emerging from Congress. Gilens and Page analyzed 1,799 policy issues in detail, determining the relative influence on them of economic elites, business groups, unions, and average citizens. Their conclusion: "The preferences of the average American appear to have only a minuscule, near-zero, statistically non-significant impact upon public policy."

According to Gilens and Page, lawmakers mainly listen to the policy demands of big business and wealthy individuals—those with the most lobbying prowess and deepest pockets to bankroll campaigns and promote their views. Before you're tempted to say "Duh," wait a moment. Gilens and Page's data come from the period 1981 to 2002. This was before the

Supreme Court opened the floodgates to big money in the *Citizens United* case, prior to super PACs, before "dark money," and before the Wall Street bailout, so it's likely to be far worse now.

You might wonder whether the average citizen ever had much power. The eminent journalist and commentator Walter Lippmann argued in his 1922 book *Public Opinion* that the broad American public didn't know or care about public policy. "It is no longer possible . . . to believe in the original dogma of democracy," Lippmann concluded. Yet as other nations succumbed to communism or fascism in subsequent years, American democracy seemed comparatively robust. American political scientists hypothesized that even though the voices of individual Americans were rarely heard, most people belonged to interest groups and membership organizations— clubs, associations, political parties, unions—whose collective voices were loud. "Interest-group pluralism," as it was called, channeled the views of individual citizens and made American democracy function. The political power of big corporations and Wall Street was offset by the power of labor unions, farm cooperatives, retailers, and smaller banks. Economist John Kenneth Galbraith dubbed it "countervailing power." These alternative power centers ensured that America's vast middle and working classes received a significant share of the gains from economic growth.

Over the last four decades, countervailing power has almost disappeared. Grassroots membership organizations have wilted because Americans have had less time for them. As wages have stagnated, most people work more hours in order to make ends meet, including the women who have streamed into the paid workforce to prop up family incomes. Similarly, union membership has plunged because corporations began busting unions—sending jobs abroad, replacing striking workers, illegally firing workers who tried to form unions, and moving to so-called right-to-work states where workers don't have to pay union dues. The disappearance of labor's countervailing power can readily be seen in the 2015–16 election cycle, when corporations and Wall Street contributed $34 to candidates from both parties for every $1 donated by labor unions and all public interest organizations combined. Business outspent labor $3.4 billion to $213 million. All of the nation's unions *together* spend about $48 million annually on lobbying in Washington. Corporate America spends $3 billion.

Other centers of countervailing power—retailers, farm cooperatives, and local and regional banks—have lost ground to national discount chains, big agribusiness, and Wall Street. Meanwhile, political parties have stopped representing the views of most constituents. As the costs of campaigns have escalated, the parties have morphed from state and local membership organizations into national fund-raising machines.

Large and growing donations to politicians do not stem from the oligarchy's inherent generosity or its abiding public spiritedness. Corporations do not fork over hundreds of millions of dollars because they love America. These expenditures are investments, and the individuals and corporations that make them expect a good return on them. The reason the American oil industry gets $2.5 billion a year from the government in special benefits, including the rights to drill for oil on public lands and take private lands for oil pipelines, has nothing to do with the public's interest in obtaining more oil. It is because Big Oil spends some $150 million a year backing pliant politicians. That $2.5 billion worth of government benefits is a remarkably good return on investment.

When JPMorgan and other big corporations donated to the Republican Party in the 2016 elections in anticipation of a giant tax cut if Republicans won, their donations were also investments, and they paid off big. As a result of that tax cut, JPMorgan would receive about $20 billion in tax savings over five years. Pfizer, whose donations to the GOP in 2016 totaled $16 million, would reap $39 billion in tax savings. GE contributed $20 million and will get back $16 billion in tax savings. Chevron donated $13 million and received $9 billion. Not even a sizzling economy can deliver anything close to the returns on political investments.

Wall Street is a major source of campaign money for both parties. In the 2008 presidential race, the financial sector ranked fourth among all industry groups giving to then candidate Barack Obama and the Democratic National Committee. His Republican opponent reaped far less. The reason politicians from both parties rely on the Street's largesse is the same reason Al Capone gave for robbing banks—that's where the money is. Connecticut Democratic senator Chris Murphy, who received $44,903 from JPMorgan in 2018, put it this way: "You spend a lot of time on the phone with people who work in the financial markets. And so you're hearing a lot about problems that bankers have and not a lot of problems that people who work at the mill in Thomaston, Connecticut, have."

The problem is not excessive greed. If you took the greed out of Wall Street, all you'd have left is pavement. The problem is the Street's excessive power. How else can you explain why the Street was bailed out with no strings attached? Or why taxpayers didn't get equity in the banks that were bailed out, as Warren Buffett did when he helped Goldman Sachs; when the banks became profitable again, taxpayers didn't reap any of the upside gains. Or why the 2010 Dodd-Frank regulatory reform law, designed to prevent a repeat of the Street's near meltdown, has itself been melted down? According to the Center for Public Integrity, the Street and other financial institutions hired roughly three thousand lobbyists to fight Dodd-Frank—more than five lobbyists for every member of Congress—and since then the Street has utilized nearly the same number to delay, weaken, or otherwise prevent its implementation.

In the latter group of lobbyists are many of the same lawmakers and congressional staff who were responsible for Dodd-Frank in the first place, drawn from both parties—including six of ten senators who retired from Congress after serving on the Senate Banking Committee and several former House members who had served on the House Financial Services Committee. In 2015, former House Financial Services Committee chair Barney Frank joined the board of directors of Signature Bank, where over the next three years he earned more than $1 million, according to regulatory filings. In January 2018, former Senate Banking Committee chair Christopher

Dodd joined the law firm of Arnold & Porter Kaye Scholer. A news release from the firm said Dodd would aid clients on issues "affecting financial services," among other policy areas.

Meanwhile, several former Obama administration officials who had led the response to the financial crisis are now working on Wall Street, including former Obama Treasury secretary Timothy Geithner, who became an executive at a private equity firm when he left the administration; Jack Lew, another former Obama Treasury secretary, who also joined a private equity firm; Obama budget director Peter Orszag, who moved into a top position at Citigroup; and former Securities and Exchange Commission chair Mary Schapiro, who became a member of the board of Morgan Stanley.

The revealing comparison is not between the career paths of Democratic and Republican officials but between people who served in Washington decades before the big money began pouring in and those who served after the deluge started. In the 1970s, only about 3 percent of retiring members of Congress went on to become Washington lobbyists. In recent years, fully half of all retiring senators and 42 percent of retiring representatives have turned to lobbying, regardless of party affiliation. This is not because more recent retirees have had fewer qualms than their predecessors about making money off their contacts and experience in government. It is because the financial rewards from corporate lobbying have grown considerably larger. "There's always been an allure of making more money when you leave Congress," explained former Democratic representative Gary L. Ackerman, who noted that some of his previous colleagues saw their pay jump to more than $1 million a year after leaving Capitol Hill. "A lot of them are very talented and entitled to it," he added.

Dimon calls "government relations" JPMorgan's "seventh line of business"—in addition to collecting credit card fees, betting on derivatives, advising clients, lending, investing, and doing deals. Dimon's seventh line has proven as lucrative as the other six, if not more so. "Government relations" is a polite phrase for influence peddling—using campaign contributions and lobbying to gain favors in Washington. Dimon has built this seventh line of business with a relish. Although in 2007 he gave himself a D for his efforts in Washington, he has since then revamped and enlarged the firm's government affairs office. He now earns an A.

JPMorgan has become the most influential Wall Street bank in Washington, not only because of Dimon's connections but also because of the bank's generosity toward Republicans and Democrats alike. In the 2018 midterms it contributed $149,908 to the Republican National Committee, $58,590 to the National Republican Congressional Committee, $70,382 to the National Republican Senatorial Committee, $115,080 to the Democratic Congressional Campaign Committee, and $108,740 to the Democratic Senatorial Campaign Committee. In the 2016 general election, it contributed $3,722,903—including $572,496 to Hillary Clinton, $246,449 to the Democratic National Committee, $187,276 to the Republican National Committee, $92,350 to the National Republican Congressional

Committee, $46,747 to the Democratic Senatorial Campaign Committee, and $36,108 to the National Republican Senatorial Campaign Committee. As I've noted, JPMorgan also maintains a platoon of Washington lobbyists. In 2018, the bank spent $5,960,000 on lobbying, placing it among the biggest corporate influencers in America. Forty-five out of its fifty-one lobbyists previously held government jobs.

The bank spent more money lobbying against Dodd-Frank than any other Wall Street firm—creating exceptions, exemptions, and loopholes that effectively allowed it to do much of what it was doing before the crisis. Then, once Dodd-Frank was enacted, Dimon and JPMorgan did more than any other bank to water it down. In December 2014 Dimon managed to get inserted into a 1,600-page bill to keep the government funded a provision repealing the portion of Dodd-Frank requiring banks to move their riskiest activities—such as derivatives trading—to entities not insured by the Federal Deposit Insurance Corporation.

The original provision had been intended to prevent taxpayers from being left holding the bag again if trades blow up, a not-unreasonable goal in light of what had occurred just a few years before. But that provision had proven costly to JPMorgan because it eliminated what amounted to free federal insurance backstopping the bank's high-risk, high-profit trading of derivatives. Its repeal was so important to JPMorgan's profits that Dimon telephoned individual lawmakers of both parties to urge them to vote for repeal, enraging House minority leader Nancy Pelosi, who charged that it was "the same old Republican formula: privatize the gain, nationalize the risk. You succeed, it's in your pocket. You fail, the taxpayer pays the bill. It's just not right."

Jamie Dimon insists that the near meltdown of 2008 was a perfect storm that will never happen again. "Most of the bad actors are gone," he told Fed chief Ben Bernanke in 2011. Therefore, he argued, there was no longer any need to crack down on the Street. But then something awkward happened. In the spring of 2012 an unassuming trader in JPMorgan's London office named Bruno Iksil accumulated such a large position on an index based on the creditworthiness of more than one hundred companies that he distorted the market. The insurance he was selling (in the form of credit-default swaps) became cheaper than the individual companies on the index. Betting that the imbalance had to correct itself at some point, hedge funds saw an opportunity to make money by taking the other side of the trade. But instead of unwinding the position and taking losses, JPMorgan's London team added to it. Global traders outside JPMorgan were stunned. "It's basic risk management," said one. "I do not see how you miss it."

They called Bruno the "London Whale." When rumors began to fly, Dimon characterized it as "a complete tempest in a teapot." Three weeks later he announced that the bank had lost $2 to $3 billion (the eventual figure would be north of $6 billion) in trades that were "poorly executed" and "poorly monitored," the result of "many errors," "sloppiness," and "bad judgment." But not to worry, he assured Wall Street and its regulators. "We will admit it, we will fix it and move on." Dimon was called before the Senate Banking Committee to explain. "We made a mistake," he admitted. "I am absolutely responsible. The buck stops with me."

The buck would not have stopped with Dimon had the London Whale swallowed the global banking system. If anything, the episode offered proof that the near meltdown of 2008 could happen again. JPMorgan was supposed to be "the port in the storm" (Dimon's words), the bank that didn't need a bailout (he repeatedly said). But less than four years after the financial crisis forced American taxpayers to bail out the Street and sent the entire American economy hurtling into the worst downturn since the Great Depression, JPMorgan recapitulated the whole debacle with the same kind of errors, sloppiness, and bad judgment, and the same excessively risky, poorly executed, and poorly monitored trades that had caused the crisis in the first place.

Dimon wants JPMorgan to grow even bigger. He believes that through economies of scale the bank could control even more of the financial industry. But what about *diseconomies* of scale—lack of adequate attention to detail, seemingly small risks that can explode if overlooked or mishandled, the hubris that often comes with large size—just the kind of errors that created the London Whale? Dimon argues that financial mergers are no different from combining Chevrolet and Buick and calling it General Motors. But financial assets are different from automobile assembly lines, which are made out of metal and bolted in concrete. During a panic, money can disappear in minutes.

How big will Congress and bank regulators allow JPMorgan to get? Much of the answer will depend on Dimon's seventh line of business—politics—which continues to reap fabulous returns.

What if anything does "corruption" mean in a system where it's legal to effectively purchase politicians' votes? In 2014, the Justice Department obtained documents showing JPMorgan was hiring the children of China's ruling elite in order to get business from Chinese government-run companies. "You all know I have always been a big believer of the Sons and Daughters program," one JPMorgan executive wrote in an email, because "it almost has a linear relationship" to winning assignments to advise Chinese companies. The documents even included spreadsheets listing the bank's "track record" for converting such hires into business deals.

It was a serious offense. But how different is bribing China's princelings, as they're called, from Wall Street's ongoing program of hiring departing Treasury officials and former members of Congress to grease the wheels of official Washington? How much worse is it than the torrent of money JPMorgan and every other major American corporation is pouring into the campaign coffers of American politicians?

The Foreign Corrupt Practices Act, which JPMorgan violated, prohibits American companies from paying money or offering anything of value to foreign officials for the purpose of "securing any improper advantage." Hiring their children was certainly something of value to China's ruling elite. Under the act, the gift doesn't have to be linked to any particular benefit to the American firm as long as it's intended to generate an advantage its competitors don't enjoy. Compared to this, corruption of American officials is a breeze. The Foreign Corrupt Practices Act is important, and JPMorgan was justly nailed for bribing Chinese officials, but why isn't there a Domestic Corrupt Practices Act? Corruption is corruption, and bribery is bribery, no matter what country or language it's transacted in.

As the system is now organized, we don't even require that American corporations disclose to their shareholders the campaign contributions they bestow on American politicians. When in 2013 Barack Obama's Securities and Exchange Commission signaled it might formally propose a rule to require corporations to disclose their political spending, the idea attracted more than 600,000 mostly favorable public comments, a record response for the agency. But the proposal mysteriously slipped off the SEC's 2014 agenda without explanation. Could that have anything to do with the fact that it was fiercely opposed by corporations and groups like the Business Roundtable?

The increasing dominance of money from the super-wealthy would be less of a problem if their attitudes were the same as those of most other Americans. The power of Democratic billionaires presumably would balance the power of Republican billionaires. But in reality the rich have quite different priorities from average Americans. Dueling billionaires are no substitute for democracy. According to a Pew Research poll, a large majority of Americans, regardless of party, are worried about jobs and wages. Yet when political scientists Benjamin Page and Larry Bartels surveyed Chicagoans with an average net worth of $14 million, their biggest concerns were the budget deficit and excessive government spending. And—no surprise—these wealthy individuals were also far less willing than were other Americans to raise taxes on the rich and more willing to cut Social Security and Medicare. They also opposed things most other Americans favored, such as increasing spending on schools and raising the minimum wage.

These wealthy respondents also differed from the rest of America in their political influence. In the previous twelve months, two-thirds had contributed (an average of $4,633) to political campaigns. A fifth had "bundled" contributions with others. That bought them the kind of political access most Americans only dream of. About half had recently initiated contact with a U.S. senator or representative, and nearly half those contacts concerned matters of narrow economic self-interest rather than broader national concern. Mind you, this is just the wealthy of one city, Chicago. Multiply it across the entire United States and you see who our elected representatives are listening to and why. The survey didn't even include the wealth and political clout of Wall Street and big corporations. Multiply the multiplier.

Between 1989 and 2009 (the latest years for which data is available), Dimon and his wife, Judy, personally donated more than $500,000 to Democratic candidates and committees.

They also contributed $48,800 to Republican candidates. They donated $4,000 to former president George W. Bush during his two presidential campaigns, as well as $2,000 each to former House minority whip Eric Cantor, Senate minority leader Mitch McConnell, and senators Mel Martinez, Richard Shelby, and John Cornyn, among others.

Dimon met Barack Obama during Obama's 2004 Senate run at a private get-together with about ten other pro-business Democrats and sent Obama's campaign $2,000, the maximum allowed. Dimon and his wife each contributed $2,000 to Hillary Clinton's 2000 Senate campaign, and each sent $2,000 to her 2006 Senate reelection campaign. In 2007, Dimon donated to then-senator Hillary Clinton $2,300, the maximum allowed. Dimon got to know Obama's Treasury secretary, Tim Geithner, when Geithner was president of the Federal Reserve Bank of New York and Dimon sat on the New York Fed's board. He got to know Rahm Emanuel, Obama's first chief of staff, when Emanuel was a senior adviser to President Bill Clinton. After Emanuel left the Clinton administration, Dimon offered him a job at Citibank. Emanuel chose instead to go with the investment banking firm Wasserstein Perella & Company, where he made $18 million in two and a half years. (Afterward, Emanuel tapped Wall Street as a major source of political funds for the Democratic Congressional Campaign Committee.) Dimon also knew Bill Daley from the Clinton administration. Obama chose Daley to succeed Emanuel as chief of staff. After Daley left the Clinton administration, Dimon hired him to be vice chair of JPMorgan and head of government relations.

. . .

In 1990, the Supreme Court sensibly defined "corruption" to include "the corrosive and distorting effects of immense aggregations of wealth that are accumulated with the help of the corporate form and that have little or no correlation to the public's support for the corporation's political ideas." After that, the high court's view of corruption became far more lenient. In 1999, in *United States v. Sun-Diamond Growers of California,* Justice Antonin Scalia, writing for the Court, interpreted an anti-bribery law so loosely as to allow corporations to give gifts to public officials, unless the gifts were linked to specific policies. Then, in the 2010 case *Citizens United v. Federal Election Commission,* the Court defined "corruption" to mean the exchange of specific money for specific votes—in other words, it's only bribery if it's specific and intentional. Writing for a majority, Justice Anthony Kennedy declared—defying all logic and reason—that "independent expenditures, including those made by corporations, do not give rise to corruption or the appearance of corruption."

Tell that to most Americans. Confidence in political institutions and actors continues to plummet in large part because most people know that wealthy people and powerful corporations are buying votes. In 1964, just 29 percent of voters believed that government was "run by a few big interests looking out for themselves." By 2013, 79 percent of Americans believed it. In Rasmussen Reports polls done in the fall of 2014, 63 percent thought most members of Congress were willing to sell their vote for either cash or a campaign contribution, and 59 percent thought it likely their own representative already had.

Corruption has become systemic, reaching deep into both political parties. While there are important differences between parties—Democratic members of Congress are far more socially liberal than Republicans and more concerned about poverty, climate change, guns, and the rights of women and minorities—neither party is committed to challenging the increasing concentration of wealth and power in America. Both have come to depend on that wealth, and therefore defer to that power. "I give money to everybody, even the Clintons, because that's how the system works," Trump said in 2016. Those might have been the most honest words ever to come out of his mouth.

CHAPTER 5

The Silence of the CEOs

JAMIE DIMON and the other members of the Business Round-table, as well as all other CEOs of major American corporations, want to be seen as national leaders, not just as wealthy CEOs of profit-seeking corporations. But in their complicity with Donald Trump they abdicated whatever moral claim to leadership they might have had.

After Trump equated white supremacists with those who protested against them in Charlottesville, Virginia, in the summer of 2017, Dimon and other major CEOs who initially had joined Trump's business advisory councils resigned from their posts. Dimon said he "strongly disagreed" with Trump, but also counseled that no one should "expect smooth sailing" in the first year of a new administration.

That was the high watermark of CEO opposition to Trump. When Trump accused the press of being "enemies of the people," Dimon and all other CEOs remained silent. When Trump claimed *The New York Times* was guilty of treason, they still said nothing. When Trump berated black athletes who were protesting police violence by not standing for the national anthem, and later told four Democratic representatives of color they should "go back home," all the CEOs were mute. When Trump used unappropriated money to begin work on his wall on the southern border, impugned the integrity of judges who disagreed with him, used his office for personal gain, played down Russia's continuing role in attacking our election system, and asked the prime minister of Ukraine to dig up dirt on his most likely 2020 opponent, Dimon and the other CEOs remained silent. When Trump ordered mass raids on immigrants, separated families at the border, held children in cages, and instructed the government to collect citizenship information on the 2020 census, the CEOs registered no concern. Not even an impeachment inquiry caused America's CEOs to voice criticism or qualms about Trump.

In these and other instances where Trump has assaulted the institutions of American democracy or fueled racism and xenophobia, the captains of American industry have remained remarkably, conspicuously, and consistently quiet. In fact, they have sung Trump's praises. Toward the end of 2018, when asked how Trump was doing, Dimon gushed, "Regulatory stuff, good." The summit with North Korea's Kim Jong-un was a "great idea." Trump's trade war with China was a smart "negotiating tactic." Dimon called the relationship between big business and the White House "active and good." Asked about Trump saying the Fed had "gone crazy," Dimon said he had "never seen a president who wanted interest rates to go up." In JPMorgan's earnings statement for the last quarter of 2018, Dimon gave Trump a shout-out for "smart regulatory policy and a competitive corporate tax system."

All the while, Dimon and the other Business Roundtable CEOs have kept their money flowing into the coffers of the Republican Party. Corporate money is vital to the GOP's continued existence. Had the CEOs threatened to cut off funding, Senate and House Republicans might have found the courage to stand up to Trump. History will show that the CEOs of America's largest corporations had the power to constrain the most dangerous, divisive, and anti-democratic president ever to occupy the Oval Office, but they chose not to use that power. One explanation for their complicity is that Trump's divisiveness is politically helpful to them. It keeps Americans fighting each other rather than discovering their common interest in fighting oligarchy. Another explanation can be found by following the money. Trump's tax cuts and frenzy of deregulation have caused corporate profits to soar. As I've noted, JPMorgan's net income for 2018 was a whopping $30.7 billion—36 percent over the previous year, more money in a single year than any American bank had ever made in history. Between the Trump inauguration and mid-2019, JPMorgan's profits rose by nearly one-third. Dimon's own compensation soared as well. So did the pay of all other CEOs. Never underestimate the power of large compensation packages to purchase scruples.

Before the vote on the tax cut, Dimon publicly predicted it would "incent business investment and job creation." He repeatedly said so—on television, in print, in speeches, in radio interviews, online, in communications with shareholders. He was the most prominent and consistent business executive to claim that Trump's tax cut would be good for America. But as I have noted, nothing of the sort occurred. The tax cut was just another giant sump pump, siphoning off more economic gains from the bottom 90 percent to the top. In June 2019, the big four—JPMorgan, Citi, Bank of America, and Wells Fargo—announced they would repurchase a combined $105 billion in shares over the year. The government's growing budget deficit, meanwhile, forced the U.S. Treasury to borrow $1 trillion in 2019 for the second straight year, which meant less federal money for schools, health care, education, and other public services.

For years the nation has been losing the taxpayer-supported public goods that are available to all. In their place has come a vast outcropping of private goods available mainly to the well-off. At the same time, America's rich have been paying less in taxes to support the common good. And more government expenditures have been finding their way into bailouts, subsidies, and government contracts going to favored industries like coal, oil, Big Agriculture, Wall Street, and industries specializing in production for the military. There is something dreadfully wrong with this picture.

A second large gift Trump delivered to Dimon and his colleagues at the Business Roundtable is deregulation. As with tax cuts, deregulation had begun four decades before, but it accelerated wildly under Trump. Dimon asserted in his 2017 letter to shareholders that regulations were costing America $2 trillion a year, or "approximately $15,000 per U.S. household annually." He lamented that "since the financial crisis, thousands of new rules and regulations have been put into place by multiple regulators in the United States and around the world." Dimon said nothing about the benefits of regulation—say, protecting the public from another financial crisis that could threaten the economy and cost millions of people their jobs, savings, and homes.

Trump obliged Dimon and other financial industry executives by defanging the Consumer Financial Protection Bureau and by filling the Federal Reserve and other agencies that are supposed to oversee banks with people eager to weaken the banking regulations that had been put in place after the 2008 financial crisis. The result has been even greater profits for the banks and more risk for the public. In 2019, Trump-appointed regulators gave JPMorgan the go-ahead to open branches in additional states as part of the bank's ambitious national expansion, and to acquire InstaMed—a medical payments technology firm—JPMorgan's biggest purchase since the financial crisis. Other big banks have joined the acquisitions race. In the first five months of 2019, they announced more mergers and acquisitions than during any full-year period since 2008.

Deregulation is another form of trickle-down economics in which gains go upward and losses trickle downward. It frees businesses to be more profitable but increases the risk the public will be harmed, fleeced, shafted, injured, or sickened by corporate products and services. After heavy lobbying by the chemical industry, Trump's Environmental Protection Agency scaled back the way the government decides whether some of the most dangerous chemicals on the market pose health and safety risks. This increases chemical industry profits but leaves the public less protected from toxins that could make their way into dry-cleaning solvents, paint strippers, shampoos, and cosmetics. If the EPA succeeds in repealing the Clean Power Plan, which set the first-ever limits on carbon pollution from U.S. power plants, wealthy shareholders of power companies will do better, but most of us will bear the risk of more carbon dioxide in the atmosphere and faster climate change. Trump's Education Department stopped investigating for-profit colleges, resulting in more profits for the for-profits but leaving many young people and their parents more vulnerable to fraud. Trump's Labor Department reduced the number of workers eligible for overtime pay and proposed allowing teenagers to work long hours in dangerous jobs that labor laws used to shield them from. Again, the result will be more profits for business and more risks borne by the rest of us.

Throughout the federal government Trump appointed industry lobbyists and executives to run agencies charged with protecting the public but who deregulated or privatized the industries they once ran or lobbied for. They will do well when they head back to the private sector, but it is unlikely that the rest of us will. We may not know for years the extent to which we are unprotected—until the next financial collapse, the next public health crisis, the next upsurge in fraud, or the next floods or droughts made worse because the National Weather Service was compromised or the EPA failed to do what it could to slow and reverse climate change.

. . .

Shortly after Trump was elected, Dimon marveled that the new president had reawakened America's "animal spirits." Other business leaders were similarly giddy. Dalio predicted that Trump would offer "a uniquely attractive environment for those who make money and/or have money," claiming that the new president would "shift the environment from one that makes profit-makers villains with limited power to one that makes them heroes with significant power." At least Dalio was correct about wealth and power.

The oligarchy may be offended by Trump's bigotry and xenophobia. It may be uncomfortable with his attacks on democratic institutions. It may cringe at his chronic lies. But it likes the money being put in its pockets as a result of his tax cuts and deregulation. That has been enough to mute its criticism. Yet for the leaders of American business to remain silent in the face of what Trump did to America makes a cruel mockery of their claims to leadership.

CHAPTER 6

The Core Contradiction

THE TYPICAL AMERICAN, as I have shown, has little wealth and has "near-zero, statistically non-significant" political power. Almost all wealth and power now reside in the oligarchy. Yet the oligarchy is not committed to the public good. It does not want to raise the wages of working Americans, reduce inequalities, guarantee all Americans access to good health care and a world-class education, or stop climate change. The oligarchy's allegiance is to corporate shareholders, and its major interest is enlarging their and its own wealth. The easiest ways to lift share values and enlarge the oligarchy's wealth are to hold down wages, roll back regulations, find ever-cheaper places around the world to produce products and services, fight unions, and secure giant tax cuts that result in less money for education, health care, and everything else most Americans need.

Don't blame CEOs or other members of the oligarchy. They're in business to make a profit and maximize their share prices, not to serve America. But they also dominate American politics and essentially run the American system, and therein lies the problem. They cannot fulfill both roles—they cannot be advocates for their corporations and simultaneously national leaders. Jamie Dimon may sincerely believe that he's a patriot before he's the CEO of JPMorgan, but we would be foolhardy to rely on that self-assessment. The difficulty is not that corporate power is beyond the control of the American government. It is that corporate power controls the American government.

As a result, Americans don't get nearly as good a deal as do the citizens of other advanced nations. Governments elsewhere impose higher taxes on the wealthy and redistribute more of it to middle- and lower-income households. Most of the citizens of other advanced nations receive free or nearly free health care, and most get free or nearly free college tuition. Americans receive neither. The United States is the only advanced nation that does not guarantee paid family leave. In Europe, the norm is three months' paid leave. At most, Americans get twelve weeks' *unpaid* leave. America is also the only advanced nation that does not guarantee paid sick days. It is the only one that does not guarantee workers any vacation at all. The European Union's twenty-eight nations guarantee at least four weeks of paid vacation.

In other advanced nations, most people who lose their jobs get more generous unemployment benefits than do Americans. Employers cannot fire workers at will, as they can here. Among the three dozen advanced countries in the Organization for

Economic Cooperation and Development, the United States has the lowest minimum wage when measured as a percentage of the median wage—just 34 percent, compared with 62 percent in France and 54 percent in Britain. The typical American worker puts in more hours on the job than Canadian, European, or Japanese workers.

American corporations distribute a smaller share of their earnings to their workers than do European or Canadian-based corporations. Top corporate executives in America make far more money than their counterparts in other wealthy countries. Consequently, inequality is far wider in the United States than it is in any other advanced country, and the American middle class is no longer the world's richest. Considering taxes and transfer payments, middle-class workers in Canada and much of Western Europe are better off than in the United States. The working poor in Western Europe earn more than do the working poor in America. Globalization or technology cannot account for these differences because all these nations face much the same international competition and deal with the same technological changes. The answer is to be found in the different organization of these countries' political-economic systems.

American corporations have no special allegiance to the United States and no responsibility for the well-being of Americans, yet they have overriding power over American politics. Power is distributed differently elsewhere. Labor unions are stronger in Europe and Canada than they are in America, able to exert pressure both at the company level and nationally. Only 6.4 percent of American private-sector workers are unionized. But 26.5 percent of Canadian workers belong to a union, as do 37 percent of Italian workers, 67 percent of workers in Sweden, and 25 percent in the United Kingdom. Most other advanced nations have parliamentary systems in which average workers are represented by at least one party that specifically advocates for them. The United States has a two-party system in which the winning party gets all of a state's electoral votes, thereby discouraging third parties. Elections in other developed nations are less affected by big money than are elections in the United States, because other nations have stricter restraints on money in politics. Governments in these nations often devise laws through tripartite bargains involving big corporations and organized labor, which further binds their corporations to their nations' workforces.

A frequent argument made by the American oligarchy is that "American competitiveness" must not be hobbled by regulations and taxes. Jamie Dimon often warns that tight banking regulations will cause Wall Street to lose financial business to banks in nations with weaker regulations—allowing "Deutsche Bank to make the better deal," in his words. He says that "if there isn't a JPMorgan straddling the globe serving clients then a Chinese bank will happily fill that role." Under Dimon's convenient logic, JPMorgan *is* America. But at the same time Dimon issues these warnings, other Wall Street bankers are warning other nations that if their bank regulations are too strict, banks located there will move more of their operations to the United States. Lloyd Blankfein, CEO of Goldman Sachs, cautioned Europeans that "operations can be moved globally and capital can be accessed globally."

One advantage of being a huge Wall Street bank is you get bailed out by the federal government when you make dumb bets. Another is you can choose where around the world to make the dumb bets. It's a win-win. Wall Street wants to keep it that way. In reality, the concept of American competitiveness is meaningless when it comes to a giant financial enterprise like JPMorgan that moves money all over the world at a keystroke. For years, the bank has been underwriting global acquisitions—a Japanese beer brewer by an Australian beer company, a steel company in the United States by a Brazilian steel company. JPMorgan doesn't care where it makes money. Its profits don't directly depend on the well-being of Americans.

Dimon used the same specious argument about American competitiveness to support the Trump tax cut. "We don't have a competitive tax system here," he warned. "Our tax system has become less competitive over the last twenty years. Everyone has improved theirs. We simply haven't." But in evaluating statements like this it's always important to look behind the pronouns. Who's "we"? What's "ours"? What's "theirs"? When Dimon talks about "competitiveness," he's really talking about the competitiveness of JPMorgan, its shareholders, and executives like himself.

"American competitiveness" is just as meaningless when it comes to big American-based corporations that make and buy things all over the world. The five hundred largest corporations headquartered in the United States are steadily becoming less American. Forty percent of their employees live and work outside the United States. A third of their shareholders are non-American. They sell and buy components and services all over the world. When GM went public again in 2010 after being bailed out by the federal government, it boasted of making 43 percent of its cars in places where labor is less than $15 an hour, while in North America it could now pay "lower-tiered" wages and benefits for new employees. The boast was directed toward Wall Street traders in an effort to boost their confidence. It was not directed toward Americans whose wages have been going nowhere.

Consider another mainstay of corporate America, GE. Two decades ago most GE workers were American. Today the majority are non-American. Over half of GE's revenue in 2018 came from abroad. According to the Commerce Department, American-based global corporations added 2.4 million workers outside the United States in the first decade of this century while cutting their American workforce by 2.9 million. Nearly 60 percent of their revenue growth has come from outside America. Apple employs 43,000 people in the United States but contracts with more than 700,000 workers abroad. It assembles iPhones in China both because wages are low there and because Apple's Chinese contractor can quickly mobilize workers from company dormitories at almost any hour of the day or night.

It is dangerous to believe that the top executives of corporations headquartered in the United States have a special allegiance to America. In July 2019, the U.S. Senate held hearings on Facebook's planned cryptocurrency, Libra. Facebook executives cautioned that the firm must be allowed to create this currency or "some other country [that is, China] will." But Facebook's motive had nothing whatever to do with stopping China or any other country from creating its own cryptocurrency. Like JPMorgan, Facebook wants to be free to make as much money as it can, wherever it can. After all, Facebook has spent much of the last decade trying to curry favor with the Chinese in hopes of getting permission to operate Facebook apps there. Evidence of Facebook's lack of allegiance to America is evident from the fact that the worldwide association it established for Libra is located in Switzerland, home of famously lax banking laws.

The real competitiveness of the United States depends on only one thing: the productivity of Americans. That in turn depends on our education, our health, and the infrastructure that connects us. The American workforce, unfortunately, is hobbled by deteriorating schools, unaffordable college tuition, decaying infrastructure, soaring health-care costs, and diminishing basic research. All of this is putting Americans on a glide path toward lousier jobs and lower wages. Big global corporations don't see it as their responsibility to fix this, and they'd rather not have to pay for any of it. Truth be told, neither would the American oligarchy. As long as they're in control of our politics, therefore, nothing gets done.

Global corporations will create jobs wherever around the world they can get the best return—where wages are lowest, regulations and taxes are minimal, or productivity is highest. But if Americans compete on the basis of lower taxes, fewer regulations, and lower wages, it's a recipe for a continuously declining standard of living. Global companies will create good, high-wage jobs in the United States only if Americans are productive enough and clever enough to summon them. Yet global companies won't make the necessary investments in American productivity, nor will they pay taxes to do so, because their allegiance is to their shareholders and not to Americans.

American companies are not just creating routine manufacturing jobs overseas. They are also creating good high-tech jobs abroad and doing an increasing amount of their research and development there: 9 percent in 1989, 20 percent today.

China's share of global research and development now tops America's. One big reason, according to the National Science Foundation, is that American firms nearly doubled their research and development investments in Asia over the last decade. China aims to create the technologies and the jobs of the future, and has been pouring money into world-class research centers designed to lure American corporations, along with their engineers and scientists. American corporations are allowed into China on the condition that they share their R&D. The Chinese are intent on learning as much as they can from American corporations and then going beyond them.

American corporations are fine with all this as long as the deals help their bottom lines. They'll do and make things in China and give the Chinese their know-how when that's the best way to boost their profits, and they'll invest in research and development around the world wherever it will deliver the largest returns. In 2017, GE announced it was increasing its investments in advanced manufacturing and robotics in China, which it termed "an important and critical market for GE." Meanwhile, Google opened an Artificial Intelligence lab in Beijing, headed by Fei-Fei Li, Google's chief scientist for AI and machine learning, who came to Google after serving as the director of Stanford University's Artificial Intelligence Lab. These moves occurred not because GE or Google is concerned about America but because these firms want to maximize the value of their shares. (Until Google employees forced the company to stop, Google was even building China a prototype search engine, Dragonfly, designed to be compatible with China's state censors.) An Apple executive told *The New York Times,* "We don't have an obligation to solve America's problems. Our only obligation is making the best product possible"—and showing profits big enough to continually increase their share price.

Donald Trump wants China to buy more goods from American corporations and stop stealing their intellectual property, as if American competitiveness were synonymous with the profits of American-headquartered corporations. He has also said he wants American companies to move their businesses out of China. Meanwhile, China is pouring money into the education of its people. In the last dozen years China has built twenty universities, each intended to become the equivalent of MIT. China is also investing in infrastructure at three times the rate of the United States.

China has a national economic strategy that's designed to maximize China. It is focused on creating more and better jobs for China and taking the lead in industries of the future, and it is achieving these goals. Forty years ago China was still backward and agrarian. Today it's the world's second-largest economy, home to the world's biggest auto industry and some of the world's most powerful technology companies. Over the last four decades, hundreds of millions of Chinese people have been lifted out of poverty.

At the core of China's economy are state-owned companies that borrow from state banks at artificially low rates. These state firms balance the ups and downs of the economy, spending more when private companies are reluctant to do so. They're also engines of China's economic growth—making the capital-intensive investments China needs to prosper, including investments in leading-edge technologies. China's planners and state-owned companies are not interested in boosting share prices. They are interested in boosting China. Since 1978, the Chinese economy has grown by an average of more than 9 percent per year. Growth has slowed recently and American tariffs could bring it down further, but it is still growing faster than almost any other economy in the world.

The United States doesn't have a national economic strategy to make necessary investments in the United States. Instead, it has a hodgepodge of tax breaks and corporate welfare crafted by American-based global corporations to maximize their profits. Big Oil gets a nice return on its political investments, as do America's biggest banks, giant military contractors, the largest food processors, the biggest private equity and hedge funds, and other beneficiaries of the American system of corruption. Meanwhile, Congress is cutting publicly supported research and development, and cash-starved states are cutting K–12 education and slashing the budgets of their great public research universities.

The Trump tax cut did little for jobs and wages but did nicely for corporate executives and big investors. As I have noted, instead of reinvesting the savings in their businesses, companies used most of it to buy back their shares of stock. In June 2019, Walmart, America's largest employer, announced it would lay off 570 employees despite taking home more than $2 billion courtesy of the Trump tax cut. In 2018 the company closed dozens of its Sam's Club stores, leaving thousands of Americans out of work. At the same time, Walmart plowed more than $20 billion into buying back shares of its own stock, which boosted the pay of Walmart executives and enriched wealthy investors but did nothing for the economy. (It should also be noted that Walmart is a global company, not adverse to bribing foreign officials to get its way. In June 2019 it agreed to pay $282 million to settle federal allegations of overseas corruption, including channeling more than $500,000 to an intermediary in Brazil known as a sorceress for her ability to make construction permit problems disappear.)

I'm not suggesting we emulate the Chinese system. What I am suggesting is that it is folly to count on American corporations and their CEOs to voluntarily create good American jobs, raise the productivity and wages of American workers, and make America the leader of the industries of the future. Rather than try to get China to change, we'd do better to try to lessen the dominance of big American corporations over

American policy. China isn't the reason half of America hasn't had a raise in four decades. The reason has more to do with where power is located in our system. The core contradiction is that Americans cannot thrive within a system run largely by big American corporations, which are not organized to promote the well-being of Americans. Oligarchy is good only for oligarchs.

PART II

The Road to Oligarchy

CHAPTER 7

The Vicious Cycle

THE ROAD TO OLIGARCHY has been paved by a relatively small number of hugely wealthy people with outsized influence over the rules of the game. For the last four decades they have used their growing power and wealth to alter the American system in ways that further enlarge their power and wealth, compounding and concentrating their dominance over the system. They have siphoned off economic gains that otherwise would have gone to the bottom 90 percent. Stagnant wages and insecure incomes for most are not the by-products of neutral economic forces but of institutions and politics caught in this vicious cycle—the consequences of a massive shift in power.

One of the most dangerously deceptive ideas is that we work and live in a free market that is neutral and natural—existing outside government, unaffected by how power is allocated in the system. We are repeatedly told that whatever inequalities and insecurities the market generates and whatever negative consequences it causes are beyond our control. Efforts to reduce inequality or insecurity are described as constraints on the market's freedom, likely to cause grave unintended consequences. In this view, if some people aren't paid enough to live on, the market has determined they aren't worth enough. If others rake in billions, they must be worth it. If millions of Americans are unemployed or their paychecks are shrinking or they work two or three part-time jobs with no idea what they'll earn next month or next week, that's just the natural outcome of market forces. If the planet's survival is endangered because of fossil fuels, nothing significant can be done about it. Government shouldn't intrude because the free market knows best. As Jamie Dimon put it, "Don't mess up the machine that creates the value so you can do these things. The economy is what gave us everything."

This is bunk. In reality, the free market is nothing but a set of rules about (1) what can be owned and traded (corporations? slaves? machine guns? nuclear bombs? babies? votes? the right to pollute?); (2) on what terms (hostile takeovers? corporate monopolies? the right to organize unions? a minimum wage? the length of patent protections?); (3) under what conditions (uninsured derivatives? fraudulent mortgages? mandatory arbitration of disputes?); (4) how to repay what's owed (debtor's prison? bankruptcy? corporate bailouts?); (5) what's private and what's public (clean air and clean water? health care? good schools?); and (6) how to pay for what's deemed to be public (corporate taxes? personal income taxes? a wealth tax?).

These rules do not exist in nature. They are human creations. Governments don't intrude on free markets. Governments organize and maintain markets. The system is created by people. The question is, *Which* people? The central issue is not more or less government. It's who is government *for*. In other words, it's all a question of power—who has it and who doesn't.

If democracy were working as it should, government officials would make the rules roughly according to what most citizens want them to be. They would also take into account the interests of the poor and of minorities, and give them a fair chance to make it as well. The system would be working for *all* of us. In a vicious cycle, though, the rules are made mainly by those with the power and wealth to buy the politicians, regulatory heads, and even the courts (and the lawyers who appear before them). As income and wealth concentrate at the top, so does political leverage.

In consequence, intellectual property rights—patents, trademarks, and copyrights—are continuously enlarged and extended. This creates windfalls for pharmaceutical, high-tech, biotechnology, and entertainment companies, which can preserve their monopolies longer than ever. It also means higher prices for American consumers, including the highest pharmaceutical costs of any advanced nation. Antitrust laws are relaxed, resulting in larger profits and greater political clout for the dominant corporations and higher prices and less leverage for workers. Financial laws and regulations instituted in the Great Depression decade of the 1930s are abandoned, allowing the largest Wall Street banks to acquire unprecedented influence over the economy. Bankruptcy laws are loosened for large corporations but tightened for homeowners and debt-laden college graduates. The largest banks and auto manufacturers get bailed out of a financial crisis, but homeowners in need of debt relief—disproportionately low-income minorities—do not.

Contract laws are altered to require mandatory arbitration before private judges selected by big corporations. Securities laws are relaxed to allow insider trading of confidential information. CEOs use stock buybacks to boost share prices and cash in their stock options. Tax laws create loopholes for the partners of hedge funds and private equity funds. They also contain special favors for the oil and gas industry. Over time, top marginal income-tax rates are lowered, corporate taxes are reduced, and estate taxes on great wealth are eliminated. Regulations that protect health, safety, and the environment are repealed, rolled back, riddled with exemptions, or simply not enforced. Public health declines. Schools in working-class and poor neighborhoods are so inadequate that the notion of equal opportunity becomes a bad joke.

The result of this vicious cycle is a giant but hidden upward distribution of income and wealth from the bottom 90 percent to the top. Another consequence, as I will show, is growing anger and frustration felt by people who are working harder than ever but getting nowhere, accompanied by deepening cynicism about our democracy. That anger, frustration, and cynicism is corroding the moral foundation of our society.

The way to end this vicious cycle is to reduce the huge accumulations of wealth that fuel it and to get big money out of politics. Alas, this cannot be accomplished when wealth and power are accumulating at the top. It's a chicken-and-egg dilemma. Yet vicious cycles have been reversed before. In the early twentieth century, progressives reclaimed our economy and democracy from the robber barons of the first Gilded Age. Wisconsin's "Fighting Bob" La Follette instituted the nation's first minimum-wage law. Presidential candidate William Jennings Bryan attacked the big railroads, giant banks, and insurance companies. President Theodore Roosevelt busted up the giant trusts. Suffragettes like Susan B. Anthony secured women the right to vote. Reformers like Jane Addams successfully pushed for laws protecting children and the public's health. Organizers like Mary Harris "Mother" Jones spearheaded labor unions. The progressive era welled up because millions of Americans saw that wealth and power at the top were undermining American democracy and stacking the economic deck. Millions of Americans overcame their cynicism and began to mobilize.

In order to reverse the vicious cycle in which we now find ourselves, it's important to understand how it began and how it has maintained its momentum. Three big systemic changes over the last forty years have reallocated power upward in the system. They are (1) the shift in corporate governance from stakeholder to shareholder capitalism, (2) the shift in bargaining power from large unions to giant corporations, and (3) the unleashing of the financial power of Wall Street. Each of these power shifts began when a few clever people discov-

CHAPTER 8

From Stakeholder
to Shareholder Capitalism

JAMIE DIMON wanted to be President Trump's Treasury secretary, according to several sources. But billionaire investor Carl Icahn preferred Steven Mnuchin for the job. Mnuchin got it. How did Icahn get his pick?

Icahn endorsed Trump for president in September 2015, barely three months after Trump announced his candidacy and long before he was considered a serious contender. "He's the only candidate that speaks out about the country's problems," Icahn explained at the time. "He's sending a message to the middle class that's getting through. How do you justify a mediocre CEO making $42 million while the guy really doing the work makes $50,000? There's no justification in a free society. In feudal times or czarist Russia you'd kill someone who tried to unseat you. Here all you have to do is vote. I don't know why anybody wouldn't vote for someone with that message."

Icahn's net worth was then $16.8 billion. Three years later, after Trump's tax cut and regulatory rollbacks, Icahn's net worth was $18.4 billion. One might well ask whether there's any justification for this in a free society.

Like Trump, Icahn can sound like a tribune of the people even though he has spent most of his career shafting people. A reporter once asked him why he kept making money when he already had more than he could ever spend. "It's a way of keeping score," he said. In *King Icahn,* a 1993 biography, author Mark Stevens describes Icahn as a "germophobic, detached, relatively loveless man," and quotes one contemporary saying, "Carl's dream in life is to have the only fire truck in town. Then when your house is in flames, he can hold you up for every penny you have." Isaac Perlmutter, the CEO of Marvel Comics and a veteran of the Israeli Army, likened dealing with Icahn to negotiating with terrorists.

Also like Trump, Icahn came to prominence in the roaring 1980s. As America's preeminent corporate raider, he was part of the inspiration for the character Gordon Gekko in the 1987 film *Wall Street.* When Oliver Stone was researching the film, he visited Icahn and borrowed one of Icahn's observations for the Gekko character: "If you need a friend, get a dog." (Icahn borrowed the phrase from Harry Truman's description of life in Washington. It's unclear whether Icahn also supplied the most memorable line in the film: "Greed, for lack of a better word, is good. Greed is right. Greed works.")

One of Icahn's other specialties has been investing in distressed debt, and Donald Trump has been among America's most distressed debtors. By the time Trump's infamous Taj

Mahal gambling casino on the New Jersey shore opened in the early 1990s, it was already deep in the red. Icahn bailed out Trump by purchasing its outstanding bonds at a steep discount.

It's no surprise that the ruthless corporate raider and ruthless real-estate developer were attracted to one another. Within days of his election, Trump asked Icahn to help him staff major government agencies. Once installed in the White House, Trump named Icahn his "special adviser" on regulatory issues. Icahn was assured he didn't have to divest any of his financial holdings, and he had no qualms about telling Trump to take actions that benefited his own companies—like rolling back environmental regulations affecting CVR Energy, an independent oil refinery in which Icahn held an 82 percent stake. In early May 2018, the Environmental Protection Agency granted Icahn's refinery a so-called financial hardship waiver, allowing it to avoid clean air laws and potentially saving Icahn millions of dollars. Icahn is not exactly a hardship case.

Icahn's raids typically involve identifying businesses whose assets are worth more than their stock value. Icahn then acquires enough shares of stock to force the company to make changes—such as laying off workers and taking on debt— that drive up its share price. He then sells his shares for a fat profit. Seeing Icahn coming, some companies have tried to fight him off, buying back his shares at a premium—a practice known as "greenmail," roughly analogous to paying ransom. Over the years, Icahn has made high-profile raids on companies such as Texaco, RJR Nabisco, and Phillips Petroleum. In 1985, after winning control of the now-defunct Trans World Airlines, he loaded the airline with more than $500 million in debt, stripped it of its assets, and pocketed nearly $500 million in profits. Before TWA went under, Icahn waged a bitter fight with the flight attendants' union. Because most attendants were women, he insisted they were not "breadwinners" and should not expect the same pay as male employees. Former TWA chair C. E. Meyer Jr. calls Icahn "one of the greediest men on earth."

Greedy or not, Icahn ushered in a systemic change in the American corporation that continues to this day. As Icahn and other corporate raiders made fortunes, CEOs began to devote themselves entirely and obsessively to maximizing the short-term values of their shares of stock in order to prevent a takeover.

Before Icahn and the corporate raiders, it was assumed that large corporations had responsibilities to all their stakeholders, not just their shareholders. "The job of management," proclaimed Frank Abrams, chair of Standard Oil of New Jersey, in a 1951 address that was typical of the time, "is to maintain an equitable and working balance among the claims of the various directly affected interest groups . . . stockholders, employees, customers, and the public at large." In November 1956, *Time* magazine noted approvingly that business leaders were willing to "judge their actions, not only from the standpoint of profit and loss but of profit and loss to the community." General Electric, the magazine noted, sought to serve the "balanced best interests" of all its stakeholders.

This was not just public relations effluvium like "corporate social responsibility" is today. In that era, CEOs of big companies earned modest sums—rarely more than twenty times that of their employees (now, they are paid more than three hundred times more). Many had spent their entire careers within their companies, sometimes working their way up from the factory floor or front line. Their companies were anchored in the same places they had been founded—GE in Schenectady, New York; Procter & Gamble, Cincinnati; Eastman Kodak, Rochester, New York; General Motors, Detroit; U.S. Steel, Pittsburgh. Other employees, from mid-level executives down to foremen and line workers, lived with them in the same communities. In a palpable sense, those CEOs were linked to those companies, the companies were linked to their employees, and all were rooted in their communities.

CEOs of that era saw themselves as corporate statesmen responsible for the common good. They were expected to be public leaders. Most had grown up during the Great Depression, when one out of four Americans was out of work and when Franklin D. Roosevelt had public backing to "try anything" to get the nation back on its feet—collaborating with big businesses in order to boost their profits (the National Recovery Administration); constraining them with tight regulations (the Securities and Exchange Acts, Glass-Steagall Act, Fair Labor Standards Act); making it easier for workers to unionize and forcing companies to negotiate (National Labor Relations Act). Many of these CEOs had served in World War II. Some had participated in the vast mobilization of American industry into war production.

At that time, the privilege and status of being the CEO of a large public company was as much a reward as the pay that went with it. CEOs were not expected to show high profits each year or to increase their companies' share prices. As paper executive J. D. Zellerbach told *Time* magazine, Americans "regard business management as a stewardship, and they expect it to operate the economy as a public trust for the benefit of all the people." Reginald Jones, CEO of GE, noted that "what will be expected of managers in the future [will be] intellectual breadth, strategic capability, social sensitivity, political sophistication, world-mindedness, and above all, a capacity to keep their poise amid the crosscurrents of change." In 1981, the Business Roundtable formally adopted a resolution noting that although shareholders should receive a good return, "the legitimate concerns of other constituencies must have appropriate attention." But starting in the 1980s, as a result of the takeovers mounted by Icahn and a few other raiders such as Michael Milken and Ivan Boesky, a wholly different understanding about the purpose of the corporation emerged. The system changed profoundly. Raiders targeted companies that could deliver higher returns to shareholders mainly by abandoning their *other* stakeholders—increasing profits by fighting unions, cutting workers' pay or firing them, automating as many jobs as possible, abandoning their communities by shuttering factories and moving jobs to states with lower labor costs, or simply moving them abroad. The raiders pushed shareholders to vote out directors who wouldn't make these sorts of changes and vote in directors who would (or else sell their shares to the raiders, who'd do the dirty work).

During the 1970s there were only 13 hostile takeovers of companies valued at $1 billion or more. During the 1980s, there were 150. Between 1979 and 1989, financial entrepreneurs like

Icahn mounted more than 2,000 leveraged buyouts, in which they bought out shareholders with money they borrowed, often at high rates, with each buyout exceeding $250 million. In the 1980s and 1990s, almost a quarter of all public corporations in the United States were at one time the target of an attempted hostile takeover opposed by a firm's management. Another quarter received takeover bids supported by management.

Few conditions change minds more profoundly than the imminent possibility of being sacked. Hence, across America, CEOs who were now threatened by being replaced by CEOs who would maximize shareholder value began to view their responsibilities differently: They would maximize shareholder value even more. The corporate statesmen of previous decades became the corporate butchers of the 1980s and 1990s, whose nearly exclusive focus was—in the meat-ax parlance that became fashionable—to "cut out the fat," "cut to the bone," and make their companies "lean and mean." By 1997 the Business Roundtable reversed the position it had taken in 1981. Now it declared the "job of business is in fact only to maximize shareholder wealth." (In August 2019, the Roundtable swung partly back to its earlier position. Later I'll discuss the meaning of this.)

Between 1981, when Jack Welch took the helm at GE, and 2001, when he retired, GE's stock value catapulted from $13 billion to $500 billion. Welch accomplished this largely by slashing American jobs and abandoning the communities GE had been rooted in. Before he became CEO, most GE employees had spent their entire careers with the company, usually at one of its facilities in upstate New York. But between 1981 and 1985, a quarter of them—100,000 in all—were laid off, earning Welch the moniker "Neutron Jack," along with the growing admiration of the business community. Between the mid-1980s and the late 1990s, GE slashed its American workforce by half again (to about 160,000) while nearly doubling its foreign workforce (to 130,000). Welch encouraged his senior managers to replace 10 percent of their subordinates every year in order to keep GE competitive. As GE opened facilities abroad, staffed by foreign workers costing a small fraction of what GE had paid its American employees, the corporation all but abandoned upstate New York.

CEOs have become so obsessed by shareholder value that Robert Goizueta, CEO of Coca-Cola, proclaimed in 1988 that he "wrestle[d] with how to build shareholder value from the time I get up in the morning to the time I go to bed. I even think about it when I am shaving." Goizueta's obsession starkly differed from the views of his predecessors, such as Coca-Cola's former president William Robinson, who in 1959 told an audience at Fordham Law School that executives should *not* put stockholders first. They should "balance the interests of the stockholder, the community, the customer, and the employee."

Over the past forty years, corporate raiders have morphed into more respectable-sounding "shareholder activists" and "private equity managers" who take over "underperforming" companies. Outright hostile takeovers have become rare, but that's only because corporate norms have changed. CEOs now run corporations only to maximize shareholder returns.

·   ·   ·

This systemic change could not have occurred without changes in laws and regulations that encouraged it. Some appeared small at the time, which is often the case with systemic change: It's not the size or visibility of specific legal or regulatory changes that count but their consequences for how the system functions. Ronald Reagan's administration looked favorably on the corporate raiders. Although the raiders' tactics might easily have been seen to violate the Securities Acts of 1933 and 1934 because of their reliance on risky loans, Reagan's Securities and Exchange Commission made no attempt to stop them. In fact, the Reagan administration's laissez-faire approach to antitrust allowed the raiders to mount acquisitions that the government would have challenged before.

By the mid-1980s, some in Congress considered possible curbs on the raiders. A bill proposed by Wisconsin senator William Proxmire, then chair of the Senate Banking Committee, aimed to curb the takeover frenzy. His bill would also have given management more leeway to protect their companies against takeovers financed by risky (junk) bonds. Beryl Sprinkel, then chair of Reagan's Council of Economic Advisors, testified against Proxmire's bill, telling the banking committee that the takeovers were making American industry healthier and the nation wealthier. "They improve efficiency, transfer scarce resources to higher valued uses and stimulate effective corporate management," he said. "The evidence is overwhelming that successful takeovers substantially increase the wealth of stockholders in target companies." The Securities and Exchange Commission also opposed Proxmire's bill, claiming it would "alter fundamentally not only the market for corporate control, but also the structure and operation of the nation's securities markets as a whole." The bill never got out of committee.

Years before, the economist Milton Friedman had urged CEOs to give up stakeholder capitalism. "What does it mean to say that 'business' has responsibilities?" he wrote in 1970; "businessmen who talk this way are unwitting puppets of the intellectual forces that have been undermining the basis of a free society these past decades." But it was really Michael Jensen, an economics professor who arrived at the Harvard Business School in 1984, who gave academic ballast to the notion that the sole purpose of the corporation should be to maximize shareholder returns. In his many papers, public lectures, and oversubscribed classes—from which generations of business school students launched careers on Wall Street and management consulting—Jensen reasoned that hostile takeovers disciplined what he termed "inefficient firms." He felt too many resources were "locked up" in unproductive ways. CEOs were too complacent, corporations employed workers they didn't need and paid them too much, companies were unnecessarily and inefficiently bound to their communities. Substantial value could be "extracted" by streamlining these operations, by which Jensen meant cutting payrolls and abandoning communities for new ones.

Jensen forgot one big thing. He overlooked those who would bear the burden of the changes he pushed for. As Jensen predicted, stockholders of targeted companies have continued to do well. That's because the so-called efficiency gains have gone to them, as well as to the raiders and top corporate executives. The costs of these maneuvers and of the obsession with maximizing share values, however, have been borne by workers who have been sacked or whose paychecks have stagnated and whose benefits have been cut and by the communities that have been left behind.

The academic conceit that workers are simply "resources" that will move to "higher valued uses" has proven to be crushingly and cruelly naïve. Human beings are not like financial resources. They do not move easily or seamlessly to different jobs and other places. They are rooted in families and communities. They have particular skills, established routines, abiding understanding of positions and roles. They depend on some degree of security, predictability, and stability. They want to be respected and valued. When "efficiency" gains go to a comparatively few people at the top, while the costs and burdens are borne by many others—as has been the case since the 1980s—the common good is not improved. It is cast to the winds.

By 2019, corporate profits had reached record levels and share prices had soared. This has been a boon to shareholders, especially the richest 1 percent of Americans, who own 40 percent of all shares of stock, and the richest 10 percent, who own 80 percent. Top corporate executives, whose pay is linked to share prices, have reaped a bonanza. Pay on Wall Street has reached jaw-dropping heights, as exemplified by Jamie Dimon's $31 million compensation package for 2018. But most Americans have not benefited. Many have lost ground. For most, wages have been flat or have declined, their jobs have become less secure, and their pensions have been turned into 401(k)s or have disappeared altogether. Abandoned communities are now scattered across the nation. Entire regions of the country have been left behind.

Executives claim they have a fiduciary obligation to maximize shareholders' returns. This argument is rubbish. It's also tautological. It assumes that shareholders are the only people worthy of executive concern. Yet as a practical matter they are not the only parties who invest in corporations or who bear some of the risk that the value of their investments might drop. All Americans are stakeholders in the American economy. Workers who have been with a firm for years develop skills and knowledge unique to it. Others may have moved their families to take a job with the firm, buying homes in the community. The community itself may have invested in roads and other infrastructure to accommodate the corporation. When a firm abandons those workers and those communities, these stakeholders lose the value of their investments. Why should no account be taken of their stakes?

Corporation after corporation began laying off workers in the 1980s without easing the often difficult transitions that followed—without providing workers with severance payments, job retraining, job search assistance, job counseling, help in selling homes the values of which predictably dropped when businesses left town, or help moving to where jobs existed; without aiding affected communities that were being jettisoned, or seeking to attract other businesses to make up for their losses of jobs and tax revenue, or finding other uses for the abandoned infrastructure of schools, roads, pipes, and real estate; without giving workers and communities sufficient advance notice so they could plan their own transitions. Absent any of this, millions of Americans were left to fend for themselves. It was a systemic change that would scar the nation for decades, contributing to rising anxiety, anger, and resentment across the land.

CHAPTER 9

The Power Shift

A SECOND SYSTEMIC CHANGE followed from the first. The move from stakeholder to shareholder capitalism altered the balance of power between corporations and workers. Shareholder capitalism demanded higher profits and higher share prices, and the easiest way to obtain them was to increase the bargaining power of corporations and reduce the bargaining power of workers. This required that antitrust laws be neutered so corporations could become large enough to raise prices and influential enough to obtain legal and regulatory changes to further boost their profits. It also required that unions be busted and the nation's labor laws be defanged. This would reduce workers' bargaining power to capture a share of the profits, leaving more for shareholders. As a result, big corporations have grown larger over the last forty years and labor unions weaker. Wages have stagnated and profits have increased. It has been a direct transfer: A steadily larger portion of corporate revenues have been siphoned off into profits and a shrinking portion to wages. A growing share of the total economy, likewise, has gone into profits and a smaller share to wages. The stock market has soared; workers have slumped.

Since the 1980s, after the federal government all but abandoned antitrust enforcement, two-thirds of all American industries have become more concentrated. Monsanto now sets the prices for most of the nation's seed corn. The government green-lighted Wall Street's consolidation into five giant banks, of which JPMorgan is the largest. It okayed airline mergers, bringing the total number of major American carriers down from twelve in 1980 to four today (American, Delta, Southwest, United), which now control 80 percent of domestic seating capacity. It let Boeing and McDonnell Douglas merge, leaving America with just one major producer of civilian aircraft, Boeing. Three giant cable companies dominate broadband (Comcast, AT&T, Verizon). A handful of drug companies control the pharmaceutical industry (Pfizer, Eli Lilly, Johnson & Johnson, Bristol-Myers Squibb, Merck).

Just five giant high-tech behemoths preside over key portals and platforms (Amazon, Facebook, Apple, Microsoft, Google), together comprising more than a quarter of the value of the entire U.S. stock market. Facebook and Google are the first stops for many Americans seeking news, and account for almost half of all advertising dollars spent in the United States. Apple dominates smartphones and laptop computers. Nearly

90 percent of all internet searches now go through Google. Amazon is the first stop for a third of all American consumers seeking to buy *anything*.

All this consolidation has inflated corporate profits, suppressed worker pay, supercharged economic inequality, and stifled innovation. Amazon has put most bookstores out of business and is rapidly eroding retail businesses on the nation's Main Streets. Google employs the world's most widely used search engine to promote its own services and Google-generated content over those of competitors, like Yelp. Facebook's purchases of WhatsApp and Instagram killed off two potential rivals. This mega-concentration of American industry has made it harder for newer firms to gain footholds. The rate at which new businesses have been formed in the United States has been halved since 1980.

In many locales workers have less choice of whom to work for, which is also holding down their wages. Corporations are imposing additional conditions on workers—such as anti-poaching, anti-compete, and mandatory arbitration agreements—which further weaken their bargaining power by making it harder for them to move to another employer.

Giant firms that dominate an industry also gain political power. They provide significant campaign contributions, have platoons of lobbyists and lawyers, and directly employ many voters. As a result, their CEOs' phone calls to members of Congress are promptly returned. Items they want included in legislation are dutifully inserted; those they don't want are scrapped. They get the tax loopholes, subsidies, bailouts, regulatory exemptions, and loan guarantees they seek. They can stop laws in their tracks. Never underestimate the monetary value of such largesse. The financial returns on political investments are among the highest in the whole system.

Amazon, the richest corporation in America, paid nothing in federal taxes in 2018. Meanwhile, it held an auction to extort billions of dollars from states and cities eager to be home to its second headquarters. It has also forced Seattle, its headquarters, to back down on a plan to tax big corporations like itself to pay for homeless shelters for a growing population that can't afford the sky-high rents caused in part by Amazon. In the fall of 2019, Amazon donated more than $1 million to the campaigns of city council candidates whom it judged to be compliant with Amazon's agenda. Facebook withheld evidence of Russian activity on its platform far longer than previously disclosed. When the news came to light, it employed a political opposition research firm to discredit critics.

The political power that flows from concentrated economic power was a central concern of the Gilded Age of the 1880s and 1890s. "Liberty produces wealth, and wealth destroys liberty," wrote Henry Demarest Lloyd in his popular 1894 book *Wealth Against Commonwealth*. "The flames of the new economic evolution run around us, and we turn to find that competition has killed competition, that corporations are grown greater than the State . . . and that the naked issue of our time is with property becoming master, instead of servant."

The field now called economics was then called political economy, and the public well understood that corporate power could undermine both the economy and democracy. Recall that this was the era of the robber barons, whose steel mills, oil rigs and refineries, and railroads laid the foundation for America's industrial might but who also squeezed out rivals who threatened their dominance, ran their own slates for office, and brazenly bribed public officials—even sending lackeys with sacks of money to be placed on the desks of pliant legislators. "What do I care about the law?" railroad magnate Cornelius Vanderbilt famously growled. "Hain't I got the power?" Forty-eight of the seventy-three men who held cabinet posts between 1868 and 1896 either lobbied for railroads, served railroad clients, sat on railroad boards, or had relatives connected to the railroads.

The public was appropriately enraged. "The enterprises of the country are aggregating vast corporate combinations of unexampled capital, boldly marching, not for economic conquests only, but for political power," warned Edward G. Ryan, chief justice of Wisconsin's Supreme Court. "Which shall rule—wealth or man; which shall lead—money or intellect; who shall fill public stations—educated and patriotic free men, or the feudal serfs of corporate capital?" Reformer Mary Lease charged, "Wall Street owns the country. It is no longer a government of the people, by the people and for the people, but a government of Wall Street, by Wall Street and for Wall Street."

Antitrust law was viewed as the means of breaking the link between the economic and political power of the new combinations. On introducing his antitrust bill in 1890, Republican senator John Sherman of Ohio thundered, "If we will not endure a king as a political power, we should not endure a king over the production, transportation, and sale of any of the necessaries of life." Sherman's bill passed the Senate 51 to 1, moved quickly through the House without dissent, and was signed into law by President Benjamin Harrison on July 2, 1890.

President Theodore Roosevelt—condemning the "malefactors of great wealth" who were "equally careless of the working men, whom they oppress, and of the State, whose existence they imperil"—used Sherman's Antitrust Act against E. H. Harriman's giant Northern Securities Company, through which Harriman dominated transportation in the northwest. As Roosevelt later recounted, the lawsuit "served notice on everybody that it was going to be the Government, and not the Harrimans, who governed these United States." President William Howard Taft broke up John D. Rockefeller's sprawling Standard Oil Trust in 1911. President Woodrow Wilson explained the danger of excessive economic and political power in his 1913 book, *The New Freedom:* "I do not expect to see monopoly restrain itself. If there are men in this country big enough to own the government of the United States, they are going to own it."

In subsequent years antitrust enforcement waxed or waned depending on the administration in office. Yet after 1980 it all but disappeared. The new view, popularized by Yale Law School professor, and subsequently judge, Robert Bork was that large corporate size produced economies of scale, which were good for consumers, and anything that was good for consumers was good for America. Political considerations became irrelevant. Power was no longer at issue. This was exactly the message that America's emerging corporate oligarchy wanted to hear. They used the façade of Bork's pinched academic analysis to justify killing off antitrust.

Today those who are most attentive to the growing concentration of American industry are big investors who are making bundles of money off it. "The single most important decision in evaluating a business is pricing power," counsels Warren Buffett, America's second wealthiest man, whose net worth as of July 2019 was $84.4 billion. Buffett's most important investment criterion isn't productivity, product quality, or innovation. He says it's "the power to raise prices without losing business to a competitor." Buffett has made his money by investing in monopolies, industries and companies surrounded by what he calls "moats" that keep out competitors. "We think in terms of that moat and the ability to keep its width and its impossibility of being crossed," Buffett explained in a Berkshire Hathaway meeting. "We tell our managers we want the moat widened every year."

That is why Buffett's firm holds close to a 10 percent stake in all four remaining major American airlines. It's also why Buffett loves Big Tech. At the end of 2018, his firm had $39.4 billion worth of Apple stock—its largest stock holding. He's also big on Amazon. And he's enamored with big Wall Street banks. Once, when asked to name his favorite bank, Buffett replied: "What's your favorite child?" As of mid-2019, his firm held about $6 billion of JPMorgan shares, and Buffett's top deputy, Todd Combs, sits on JPMorgan's board.

Buffett has been considered the conscience of American

capitalism because he wants the rich to pay higher taxes. "Stop coddling the super-rich," he says. He claims it's "unfair" that the tax code requires him to pay no more than about 0.002 percent of his wealth in taxes each year. Democrats even named a tax-fairness plan the "Buffett rule." (In 2018, the Trump tax cut saved Buffett's businesses $37 billion.)

But Buffett's investment strategy is indirectly taking money out of the pockets of average Americans. As I've explained, the sky-high profits at JPMorgan and the other banking behemoths on the Street are due to their being too big to fail, along with their political power to keep regulators at bay. Similarly, high profits at the four remaining major American airlines come from inflated prices, overcrowded planes, overbooked flights, and weak unions. High profits of Big Tech come from wanton invasions of personal privacy, the weaponizing of false information, and a widening moat that's discouraging innovation.

In short, moats are good for profits and big investors but not good for most workers or consumers. If Buffett really wanted to be the conscience of American capitalism, he would be a crusader for breaking up large concentrations of economic power, for filling in the moats. But he is making big money off those moats. His huge wealth and the widening gap in wealth between him and other Americans is directly connected to the power shift from average Americans to moated corporations.

Power has shifted in exactly the opposite direction for workers. By the mid-1950s, 35 percent of all private-sector workers in the United States were unionized. Today, 6.4 percent of them are.

Starting in the 1980s, and with increasing ferocity since then, private-sector employers have fought unions. Surely Ronald Reagan's decision to fire the nation's air-traffic controllers, who went on an illegal strike, signaled to private-sector employers that fighting unions was legitimate. But it was really the wave of hostile takeovers, the shift from stakeholder to shareholder capitalism, that pushed employers to crush unions. Payrolls are typically 70 percent of a corporation's costs. The most direct way to raise profits and share prices is to cut payroll costs. The first step was to bust unions.

Corporations have replaced striking workers with non-union workers. Previously, when management was responsible to all stakeholders, workers who went on strike typically got their jobs back as soon as a strike was settled. Shareholder capitalism changed this radically. Now, striking workers often lose those jobs forever. As *Fortune* magazine observed in 1985, "Managers are discovering that strikes can be broken, that the cost of breaking them is often lower than the cost of taking them, and that strike-breaking . . . doesn't have to be a dirty word." Corporations have also threatened to move jobs overseas if workers don't agree to pay cuts. In 1988, Jack Welch's General Electric threatened to close a factory in Fort Wayne, Indiana, that made electrical motors and to relocate it abroad unless workers agreed to a 12 percent pay cut. The head of GE's motor division warned that "there's a bunch of guys in Thailand, Korea, and Brazil who get up every morning and try to figure out how to eat your lunch and take your market share." The Fort Wayne workers agreed to the pay cut. Jim Daughtry, a leader of the factory's union, said, "It used to be that companies had an allegiance to the worker and the country. Today, companies have an allegiance to the shareholder. Period."

Corporations have fired workers who try to organize, a move that's illegal under the National Labor Relations Act but happens all the time because the penalty for doing so—restoring fired workers to their jobs along with back pay—is small relative to the profits that come from discouraging unionization. Corporations also mount campaigns against union votes, warning workers that unions will make them less competitive and thereby threaten their jobs. All the while, corporations have been relocating to states where so-called right-to-work laws bar unions from requiring dues from workers they represent, which effectively strips unions of any power. The Supreme Court, in an opinion delivered by the court's five Republican appointees, has extended right-to-work to public employees' unions.

The pressure to crush unions hasn't come from globalization or automation. Other developed nations, facing the same international competition and with access to the same technologies, have maintained far higher levels of unionization along with high wages and benefits. As former *New York Times* labor correspondent Steven Greenhouse has observed, "In no other industrial nation do employers fight so hard to defeat, indeed quash, labor unions." The pressure has come from corporate raiders and their more recent incarnations, private equity and hedge fund managers, demanding ever higher profits. Institutional investors (the managers of mutual funds, insurance funds, pension funds, endowments, and private equity funds) are just behind them, rooting them on. As power has shifted from workers to them, many of these investors and financial managers have become fabulously wealthy.

Meanwhile, as unions have shrunk, so has their political power. In 2009, even with a Democratic president and Democrats in control of both houses of Congress, unions could not muster enough votes to enact a simple reform that would have unionized workplaces as soon as a majority of employees signed pro-union cards. President Obama didn't fight for this. Some Democrats, threatened by groups like the Business Roundtable, wouldn't vote for it. When the legislation was introduced, 180 business executives descended on Capitol Hill to meet with swing senators. Corporations ran $1 million worth of television ads against the bill in Nebraska alone in order to pressure one vacillating Democrat, Nebraska senator Ben Nelson, to vote no. He obliged.

Unions have become even weaker at the state level. Anti-union right-to-work laws were enacted in Indiana in 2011, Michigan in 2012, Wisconsin in 2015, West Virginia in 2016, and Kentucky in 2017. Democrats in these traditional union states barely fought back. As political commentator Thomas Edsall observed, "A paradox of American politics is that Republicans take organized labor more seriously than Democrats do. The right sees unions as a mainstay of the left, a crucial source of cash, campaign manpower, and votes. . . . If Republicans and conservatives place a top priority on eviscerating labor unions, what is the Democratic Party doing to protect this core constituency? Not much." The wealth and power of the new American oligarchy has overwhelmed the Democratic Party almost as much as it has the Republican.

.　　.　　.

This great shift in bargaining power from workers to corporations and their shareholders has pushed a larger portion of national income into profits and a lower portion into wages than at any time since World War II. Most of these profits are going into higher share prices (fueled by share buybacks) and higher executive pay rather than new investment. The declining share of total U.S. income going to the bottom 90 percent over the last four decades correlates directly with this decline in unionization. No other change in the system provides as clear a relationship. Meanwhile, and for the same reason, the rising share of total income going to the richest Americans is inversely related to the share of the nation's workers who are unionized. The American economic pie continues to grow, but most workers are getting only crumbs.

Most of the increasing value of the stock market has come directly out of the pockets of American workers. Three researchers—Daniel Greenwald at MIT's Sloan School of Business, Martin Lettau at Berkeley, and Sydney Ludvigson at NYU—found that "from 1952 to 1988, economic growth accounted for 92 percent of the rise in equity values," but that from 1989 to 2017, economic growth was responsible for just 24 percent of the rise. Most of the increase in share values has come from "reallocated rents to shareholders and away from labor compensation."

America's shift from farm to factory was accompanied by decades of bloody labor conflict. The shift from factory to office and other sedentary jobs created other social upheaval.

The more recent power shift from workers to large corporations and their shareholders—and consequentially, the dramatic widening of inequalities of income, wealth, and political
power—has happened far more quietly, but it has had a more
unfortunate and more lasting consequence for the system:
an angry working class vulnerable to demagogues peddling
authoritarianism, racism, and xenophobia.

CHAPTER 10

The Last Coping Mechanism

THE THIRD SYSTEMIC CHANGE followed from the first two. Wall Street was deregulated. To understand the significance of this, you need to understand why Americans accepted stagnant wages from 1980 until the financial crisis of 2008. They honed several coping mechanisms that allowed them to behave as though they were still taking home the same share of total income as before, and to spend as if nothing had substantially changed. It wasn't until Wall Street blew up in 2008 that the last of these coping mechanisms was exhausted, and America woke up to what had happened.

Coping mechanism # 1: Women move into paid work. Starting in the late 1970s, and escalating after 1980, women went into paid work in large numbers. For the relatively small sliver of women with four-year college degrees, this was the result of wider educational opportunities and new laws against gender discrimination that opened professions to them. But the vast majority of women who migrated into paid work did so in order to prop up family incomes as the wages of male workers stagnated or declined. The changing nature of work—from heavy manufacturing to services—opened jobs that demanded less brute strength, and the use of the contraceptive pill gave women more control over when, if, and how many babies they'd conceive, thereby allowing them to put more time and energy into paid work.

This transition has been one of the most important social and economic changes to occur over the last four decades. It has reshaped American families and challenged traditional patterns of child-rearing and child care. In 1966, 20 percent of mothers with young children worked outside the home. By the late 1990s, 60 percent did. For married women with children under the age of six, the transformation went from 12 percent in the 1960s to 55 percent by the late 1990s.

By the late 1990s, families reached the limit, a point of diminishing returns where the cost of hiring others to help in the running of a household or to take care of the children, or both, exceeded the apparent benefits of the additional income. This led families to the next coping mechanism.

Coping mechanism # 2: Everyone works longer hours. What families failed to get in wage increases they made up for in work increases. By the mid-2000s, it was not uncommon for men to work more than fifty hours a week and women to work more than forty. Professionals put in more billable hours. Hourly workers relied on overtime. A growing number of people took on two or three jobs, each demanding twenty or more hours. Americans now work an average of 1,780 hours a year. That's 70 hours a year more than the Japanese, 200 hours (five workweeks) more than British workers, 266 hours (six and a half workweeks) more than French workers, and 424 hours (ten and a half workweeks) more than German workers.

How did women and men work such long hours and also take care of their families, maintain their homes? Not easily. Many did it in shifts. I have an acronym for such families— DINS, "double income, no sex." Here, too, though, Americans seemed to have reached a limit. Even if they could find additional work, they couldn't find any more time. This led to the third coping mechanism.

Coping mechanism #3: Draw down savings and borrow to the hilt. After exhausting the first two coping mechanisms, the only way Americans could keep consuming as before was to save less and go deeper into debt. During the three decades after World War II, the American middle class saved about 9 percent of their after-tax income each year. By 2008, they saved only 2.6 percent. Meanwhile, household debt exploded. Between the end of World War II and 1980, debt had averaged around 50 to 55 percent of annual after-tax income (including what people owed on their mortgages). After 1980, debt took off. In 2001, Americans owed as much as their *entire* after-tax income. The borrowing still didn't stop, especially after the Federal Reserve Board lowered interest rates and made borrowing easier. By 2007, the typical American household owed 138 percent of its after-tax income.

Americans borrowed from everywhere. Credit card solicitations flooded mailboxes; many American wallets bulged with dozens of cards, all amassing larger and larger debt loads. Auto loans were easy to come by. Students and their families went deep into debt to pay the costs of college. Far and away the largest borrowing was to buy homes. Mortgage debt exploded. As housing values continued to rise, homes doubled as ATMs. Consumers refinanced their homes with even larger mortgages and used their homes as collateral for additional loans. As long as housing prices continued to rise, it seemed a painless way to get additional money. (In 1980 the average home sold for $64,600; by 2006 it went for $246,500.) Between 2002 and 2007, American households extracted $2.3 trillion from their houses, putting themselves ever more deeply into the hole.

This last coping mechanism came to an abrupt end in 2008, when the housing and debt bubbles burst. Only then did Americans begin to realize what had happened to them, and to the system.

If any single person was responsible for the end of the last coping mechanism it was the investment banker Sandy Weill. Jamie Dimon began working for Weill in 1982. Over the next sixteen years, the combination of Dimon's number-crunching and Weill's salesmanship generated a series of hugely profitable bank mergers, culminating in 1998 with the $70 billion merger of Travelers Insurance and Citibank to form Citigroup. The duo's business strategy freed traders to make large, risky bets with other people's money—bets that delivered gigantic bonuses when they turned out well, but ultimately cost mil-

had recently been acquired by a home builder named Charles Keating, Greenspan dubbed Lincoln's management "seasoned and expert in selecting and making direct investments." The thrift failed in 1989, costing taxpayers around $2 billion. "Of course I'm embarrassed," Greenspan later told a reporter. "I don't want to say I'm distressed but the truth is I really am." (It was language he'd repeat after the 2008 financial crisis, when he told Congress he was "very distressed" by the failure of the market to discipline itself.) After the collapse of the hedge fund Long-Term Capital Management in 1998, Greenspan again insisted government should not tighten regulation of the banks that funded the hedge fund's bets nor the derivatives that allowed the hedge fund to lose so much money so quickly.

After Citicorp announced its merger with Travelers in 1998, Weill lobbied Congress and the Clinton administration— particularly Treasury secretary Robert Rubin—to repeal what remained of Glass-Steagall. Weill even phoned Bill Clinton personally. Other big banks pitched in with $300 million worth of lobbying on the issue, using the same dubious argument of national competitiveness. Some members of Congress bought it. "The future of America's dominance as the financial center of the world" was at stake, claimed Democratic senator Charles Schumer. Finally, in November 1999, the Financial Services Modernization Act was enacted and signed into law, tearing down the Glass-Steagall wall. Supporters hailed the move as the long-overdue demise of a Depression-era relic. Critics (including yours truly) predicted it would release a monster. The critics were proven correct. The repeal of Glass-Steagall transformed the American system, turning Wall Street into a giant and unfettered betting parlor.

In 2007, former Fed governor Edward Gramlich lamented that the mortgage marketplace was "like a city with a murder law, but no cops on the beat." Yet Dimon, Weill, Greenspan, Rubin, and others argued there was no need for concern. For years thereafter, a four-foot-wide hunk of wood hung in Weill's office on the forty-sixth floor of the General Motors Building in Manhattan, etched with his portrait and the words "The Shatterer of Glass-Steagall."

Shortly after Brooksley Born became head of the Commodity Futures Trading Corporation, a government agency charged with regulating markets in futures and options, in August 1996 she became curious about credit derivatives—bets on whether loans would be repaid. She didn't understand why the derivative market had to be hidden and why the industry was so opposed to record-keeping or reporting. In early 1998, after her staff began to prepare a tentative first step toward transparency, Born was summoned to a meeting with Rubin, Alan Greenspan, and Arthur Levitt, chair of the SEC, who told her to drop the issue. She did not. After the Clinton administration asked Congress to suspend her rule-writing authority, Congress barred the government from regulating large portions of the market in derivatives. Years later, Rubin said he favored making derivatives "subject to comprehensive and higher margin limits" but did not support doing it in the way Born wanted, which he called "strident." Clinton said he raised concerns about derivatives with Greenspan. "I should have aired the debate we had in private in public," he admits, "and at least raised the red flag."

During my years in Clinton's cabinet I worked closely with Rubin and found him to be thoughtful, intelligent, and self-deprecating (he often began sentences with "in my humble opinion . . ."). He and I didn't see eye to eye on many issues (I thought he worried excessively about the budget deficit; he thought I was too eager to spend money on education and health care), but our disagreements were never personal. We often dined together at the Jefferson Hotel, where Rubin resided. I found him to be socially liberal, genuinely concerned about the poor, and committed to equal opportunity. But he didn't want to talk about wealth and power. When I used the term "corporate welfare" in a speech, he almost blew a gasket.

As secretary of labor, I traveled a great deal across America—to the industrial Midwest, to the South, to the farm belt, to the Pacific Northwest, to California's Central Valley. Everywhere I went, I met families who were working harder than ever but growing less economically secure. The Clinton administration tried to make things better for them. We raised the minimum wage. We guaranteed workers time off from their jobs (although without pay) in the event of family or medical emergencies. We tried for universal health care. We offered students from poor families better access to college. We expanded a refundable tax credit for low-income workers. We tried tying executive compensation to company performance. All these policies were helpful but frustratingly small in light of the systemic changes that were occurring as a result of the move from stakeholder to shareholder capitalism, the shift in power from labor unions to corporate monopolies, and, we would eventually learn, the deregulation of Wall Street.

Federal Reserve chair Greenspan insisted that Clinton cut the federal budget deficit rather than deliver on his more ambitious campaign promises, and Greenspan reciprocated by reducing interest rates. By the late 1990s, the economy was recovering so quickly and unemployment was so low that middle-class wages started to rise a bit for the first time in two decades. The rise, however, was propelled by an upturn in the business cycle rather than any enduring change in the system, so it turned out to be a blip. Once the economy cooled, most family incomes were barely higher than before. And when the bubble burst, all hell broke loose.

In 1999, Weill and Dimon parted ways. "The problem was . . . he wanted to be C.E.O. and I didn't want to retire," Weill said of Dimon. A few months later, after the Glass-Steagall Act was repealed and Rubin stepped down as Clinton's Treasury secretary, Weill recruited Rubin to be chair of Citgroup's executive committee and, briefly, chair of its board of directors.

Between 1980 and 2008, as Wall Street was deregulated and unleashed, more than $6.6 trillion of wealth was transferred to financial firms in the United States. The economy turned from making things to making financial instruments. Product entrepreneurs were replaced by financial entrepreneurs. Even nonfinancial companies found ways to make money from financial products. Financial divisions of major corporations (such as GE Capital) became larger than their product divisions. Wall Street's financial tentacles spread to credit cards, lines of credit, college-savings plans and portfolios, pensions, and an ever-larger array of home mortgages. Finance became the epicenter of the American economy.

Then came the financial crisis of 2008.

In the run-up to the crisis, Citigroup was a leader in packaging risky mortgages and reselling them to unwary investors. On November 19, 2008, as its finances were rapidly deteriorating, Rubin called Treasury secretary Hank Paulson, who years before had succeeded Rubin as chair and CEO of Goldman Sachs. According to Paulson's memoir, *On the Brink*, Rubin told him that "short sellers were attacking" Citigroup's stock, which was "sinking deeper into the single digits." Rubin "rarely called me," Paulson wrote, so the "urgency in his voice that afternoon left me with no doubt that Citi was in grave danger." The federal government injected $45 billion of taxpayer money into Citigroup and guaranteed some $300 billion of illiquid assets. The government ended up with a 27 percent stake in the corporation. After the stake was finally sold, taxpayers came out ahead. But by then millions of Americans had lost their jobs, homes, and savings in the process. And the biggest banks on Wall Street emerged with a too-big-to-fail premium.

Rubin told *The New York Times* in April 2008 that he didn't "feel responsible, in light of the facts as I knew them in my role. Clearly, there were things wrong. But I don't know of anyone who foresaw a perfect storm, and that's what we've had here." (I saw Rubin briefly toward the end of 2008. When I asked him about the financial crisis, he described it in the same terms—"a perfect storm.") He elaborated in testimony before the Financial Crisis Inquiry Commission in March 2010. "In the world of trading, the world I have lived in my whole adult life, there is always a very important distinction between what you could have reasonably known in light of the facts at the time and what you know with the benefit of hindsight," he said. Phil Angelides, the FCIC's co-chair, was "disappointed" with Rubin's testimony. "I didn't see him stepping forward and accepting the responsibility of the disaster that Citigroup was, and for the impact it had on the taxpayers and our financial system. . . . I just don't think you can be in that kind of leadership position, get paid more than $115 million, and ultimately disclaim any responsibility for the fate of the ship you helped captain."

"Listen, nobody's perfect," says Sandy Weill. "I'm sure you've heard all sides." Weill calls Rubin "extremely" helpful to him during his years at Citi, but Weill could not account for what happened after his own departure from the bank in October 2003. (Weill remained nonexecutive chair of the Citigroup board until April 2006.) "Unfortunately, something happened that was not very pleasant for a lot of people and not very pleasant for a lot of people that worked for the company. It was very sad." Sheryl Sandberg, now the chief operating officer of Facebook, who worked at the Treasury Department under Rubin after she graduated from Harvard Business School in 1995, suspects Rubin was scapegoated for events he could not possibly have controlled. "My own view is that, look, these have been hard times, and people need people to blame. It doesn't mean they blame the right people," she said.

When he looks back on the years leading up to the financial crisis, Jamie Dimon believes that he was more prudent than the top executives of the other big banks. "As a result of our steadfast focus on risk management and prudent lending, and our disciplined approach to capital and liquidity management, we were able to avoid the worst outcomes experienced by others in the industry," he told the Financial Crisis Inquiry Commission in January 2010.

Yet between 2007 and 2009, JPMorgan racked up a remarkable $51 billion of losses from faulty mortgages, unpaid credit cards, and other bad loans. Dimon had driven the bank to undertake too many risky mortgages. At the end of 2007, even after JPMorgan had taken a $1.3 billion write-down on bad loans, Dimon told analysts it was planning to add as much as $20 billion more in mortgages from risky borrowers. Mortgage applicants weren't even required to document their income— they could just assert it. As I have noted, JPMorgan subsequently reached a then record $13 billion settlement with the Department of Justice, which documented the bank's role in underwriting fraudulent securities leading up to the 2008 crisis. The Justice Department accused the bank of, among other things, mounting "a fraudulent and deceptive scheme to package and sell residential mortgage-backed securities." It alleged that the bank knew that "many of these loans were tainted with fraud" and "knowingly misrepresented" that the loans met its underwriting guidelines, even though "they clearly did not," and that "these fraudulent misrepresentations" cost investors "to suffer billions of dollars in losses."

Dimon admitted he had underestimated the severity of the crisis. "We still found ourselves having to tighten our underwriting of subprime mortgage loans six times through the end of 2007," he wrote. "Yes, this means our standards were not tough enough the first five times."

As of 2019, about 355 bankers, mortgage lenders, real-estate agents, and borrowers had been convicted of crimes related to the financial crisis, but they were all small fry. No major executives of the largest financial firms went to jail. The total number of convictions was only about a third the number of convictions after the much smaller savings-and-loan crisis of the 1980s.

Since the financial crisis, a number of elder statesmen have pushed to have Glass-Steagall reinstated in some form. In 2009, John S. Reed, who served with Weill as co-CEO of Citigroup from 1998 to 2000, apologized for creating a lumbering giant that needed multibillion-dollar bailouts from the government. In an October 2009 letter to *The New York Times*, he wrote that "some kind of separation between institutions that deal primarily in the capital markets and those involved in more traditional deposit-taking and working-capital finance makes sense." Richard Parsons, a former Citigroup board chair, conceded that "what we saw in the 2007–2008 crash was the result of the throwing off of Glass-Steagall." Two other major figures in the fight to repeal Glass-Steagall—Philip Purcell, the former chief executive of Morgan Stanley, and David H. Komansky, the onetime leader of Merrill Lynch—have expressed similar regrets.

Even Sandy Weill confessed that Glass-Steagall had to be resurrected. "What we should probably do is go and split up investment banking from banking. . . . Have banks do something that's not going to risk the taxpayer dollars, that's not going to be too big to fail."

Dimon, on the other hand, still doesn't see any need to return to Glass-Steagall. He doesn't think big banks like JPMorgan are too big or that their commercial deposits should be shielded from their betting practices. Quite the contrary: He thinks the biggest financial institutions should be allowed to grow bigger and commingle money even more. Dimon continues to claim that giant banks like his can be managed so as to avoid any risk to taxpayers. "There's huge strength in this company that units get from each other," he says. Splitting up JPMorgan would be "very short-sighted."

Today, the financial sector of the U.S. economy is larger than ever. Americans now turn over $1 out of every $12 of the entire economy to it. In the 1950s, bankers took only $1 out of every $40. The third systemic change—financial deregulation—allowed the bankers to run wild. They're still on the run.

When the debt and housing bubbles burst in 2008, most Americans woke up to the startling reality that they could no longer afford to live as they *had* been living, nor as they thought they *should* be living relative to the lavish lifestyles of those at the top, nor as they *expected* to be living given their continuing aspirations for a better life, nor as they assumed they *could* be living, given how large the economy had grown, nor as they assumed they *would* be living given what they experienced in the three decades after World War II.

Between 1999 and 2018, the United States economy grew 48 percent, but the typical household's income did not grow at all, and the bottom half of America ended up with less wealth than it had before the financial crisis. The richest 1 percent, however, ended up with twice as much wealth as it had before the financial crisis, and the richest 0.1 percent, with three times as much.

The three systemic changes I have outlined—from stakeholder to shareholder capitalism, from unionized workers to corporate monopolies, and from regulation of Wall Street to letting the Street run wild—profoundly altered the American system. It created a jaw-droppingly wealthy and powerful oligarchy. It shafted just about everyone else.

CHAPTER 11

The Triumph of the Oligarchy

DIG UNDER THE SURFACE of the system and you see individuals making deals that generated billions for themselves—such as Carl Icahn's corporate raids, Jack Welch's attacks on GE's workers and unions, Warren Buffet's investments in corporations with moats, and Sandy Weill's and Jamie Dimon's unfettered financial supermarkets and betting parlors.

Dig deeper and you see how these deals depended on seemingly small changes in laws and regulations, such as preventing companies from defending themselves from raiders, neutering antitrust enforcement, imposing small fines on corporations for firing union organizers, refusing to regulate derivatives, and dismantling Glass-Steagall.

Bore still deeper and you see a vicious cycle in which, starting around 1980, wealth and power began concentrating among a relatively small group at the top, giving them increasing political clout to get changes in laws and regulations that concentrated their wealth and power even more.

Look at the shifting tectonic plates under all this and you view the profound shifts in the allocation of power that brought us the system we have today. The first three decades after World War II featured a growing middle class, a steadily more inclusive democracy, and a nation beginning to grapple with problems like poverty, inequality of opportunity, and environmental decay. African Americans and women slowly gained footholds in the system. Mass production begat mass consumption, and mass consumption demanded steady jobs with good wages. This balance relied on strong unions, a government willing to regulate corporations, and large corporations rooted in their communities and responsible for the well-being of their employees and neighbors as well as shareholders.

In the last forty years, the opposite has occurred: The middle class has shrunk, democracy is too often malfunctioning, and the nation has turned its back on climate change, poverty, widening inequality, and the evils of racism and xenophobia. As I've said, the economy doesn't have to be a zero-sum game in which winners do better only to the extent losers do worse. But *power* is necessarily a zero-sum game. Certain people possess it only to the extent other people don't. Some people gain it only when others lose it. The connection between the economy and power is critical. As power has concentrated in the hands of a few, those few have grabbed nearly all the economic gains for themselves.

The oligarchy has triumphed not because Carl Icahn, Jack Welch, Warren Buffett, Sandy Weill, Alan Greenspan, Robert

Rubin, Jamie Dimon, or anyone else conspired to make it happen. I doubt any of them thought about the system as a whole. They triumphed because *no one* paid attention to the system as a whole—to the consequences of the shifts from stakeholder to shareholder capitalism, from large unions to giant corporations, and from regulated to unfettered finance. The choices that the American public *assumed* were at stake—the so-called political right versus left, Republican versus Democrat, free market versus government, efficiency or inefficiency, national competitiveness or lack thereof, corporate responsibility or irresponsibility, socialism or capitalism—distracted us from the more fundamental questions about power: Who was gaining it? Who was losing it? Were we satisfied with the results? Through it all, Americans have clung to the meritocratic tautology that individuals are paid what they're worth in the market, without examining changes in the legal and political institutions that define the market. This tautology is easily confused with a moral claim that people *deserve* what they are paid. Yet this claim is meaningful only if the system's legal and political institutions are morally just. It has lured us into thinking nothing can or should be done to alter what people are paid because the market has decreed it. By this logic, the oligarchy is natural and inevitable.

Wealth is not like income. Income is payment for work. Wealth keeps growing automatically and exponentially because it is parked in investments whose value compounds over time. Because of this, today's concentration of wealth could come to resemble the kind of dynasties common to European aristocracies in the seventeenth and eighteenth centuries. We're already at a point where many of today's super-rich have never done a day's work in their lives. Six out of the ten wealthiest Americans alive today are heirs to prominent fortunes.

The three wealthiest families in America today are the Waltons of Walmart, the Mars candy family, and the Koch family, heirs to the energy conglomerate Koch Industries. Since 1982, the combined wealth of these three families has grown nearly 6,000 percent, adjusted for inflation. Over the same period, the typical household's wealth dropped 3 percent. The Walmart heirs alone have more wealth than the bottom 42 percent of Americans combined. Today, the Walmart family fortune grows by $70,000 per minute, $4 million per hour, $100 million per day.

Rich millennials will soon acquire even more. America is on the cusp of the largest intergenerational transfer of wealth in history. As wealthy boomers expire over the next three decades, an estimated $30 trillion will go to their children. Those children will be able to live off of the income these assets generate, and then leave the bulk of the assets—which in the intervening years will have grown more valuable—to their own heirs, tax-free. After a few generations of this, almost all of the nation's wealth will be in the hands of a few thousand families.

Dynastic wealth runs counter to the ideal of America as a meritocracy. It makes a mockery of the notions that people earn what they're worth in the market and that economic gains should go to those who deserve them. It puts economic power into the hands of a relatively small number of people who have never worked but whose investment decisions have a significant effect on the nation's future. It creates a self-perpetuating aristocracy that is antithetical to democracy. Dynastic wealth also magnifies race and gender disparities. Because of racism and sexism, women and people of color not only earn less, they have saved far less—which is why the racial wealth gap and gender wealth gap are huge and growing.

As I have noted, the last time America faced anything comparable to the current concentration of wealth was at the turn of the twentieth century. Then, President Theodore Roosevelt warned that "a small class of enormously wealthy and economically powerful men, whose chief object is to hold and increase their power" could destroy American democracy. Roosevelt's answer was to tax wealth. The estate tax was enacted in 1916 and the capital gains tax in 1922. Since that time, both have been eroded. As the rich have accumulated greater wealth, they have also amassed more political power, and they've used that political power to reduce their taxes.

Even as the American middle class shrinks, America now has more billionaires than at any time in its history. There are basically only four ways to accumulate a billion dollars, and none of them is a product of so-called free market. They all depend on how the system has become organized.

One way to make a billion is to exploit a monopoly. Jeff Bezos is worth $110 billion. You might say he deserves it because he founded and built Amazon. But, as I have pointed out, Amazon is a monopoly with nearly 50 percent of all e-commerce retail sales in America (and e-commerce is gaining the lion's share of all retail sales). Consumers have few alternatives. Nor do many suppliers who sell through Amazon; for the first twenty-five years of its existence, Amazon wouldn't let them sell at a lower price anywhere else. Amazon's business is protected by patents granted to Amazon by the U.S. government and enforced by government. If we had tough antimonopoly laws, and if government didn't grant Amazon so many patents and extend them for such a long time, Bezos would be worth far less. The same applies to people like George Lucas, Oprah Winfrey, or any other figure whose brands, ideas, or creations depend on patents, copyrights, and trademarks—intellectual property laws that have been dramatically extended in recent decades. If these were shortened, these people would be worth far less, too.

A second way to make a billion is to get insider information unavailable to other investors. The hedge-fund maven Steven A. Cohen is worth an estimated $12.8 billion. According to a criminal complaint filed by the Justice Department, insider trading at Cohen's SAC Capital was "substantial, pervasive, and on a scale without known precedent in the hedge fund industry." Eight of Cohen's present or former employees pleaded guilty or were convicted for using insider information. Cohen got off with a fine, changed the name of the firm, and apparently is back in the game.

A third way to make a billion is to pay off politicians. The Trump tax cut was estimated to save Charles and David Koch—each of whose net worth was estimated to be about $50 billion—and their Koch Industries $1 billion to $4 billion a year, not even counting tax savings on offshore profits and a shrunken estate tax. The Kochs and their affiliated groups spent an estimated $20 million lobbying for the Trump tax cut, including major donations to politicians. Not a bad return on investment: More than a billion dollars a year back for only $20 million put in. Koch Industries has also been a major beneficiary of government programs to fill the Strategic Petroleum Reserve, provide roads and access to virgin growth forests, use eminent domain to build pipelines, and profit off federal lands.

A fourth way to be a billionaire is to get the money from rich parents or relatives. As I've noted, about 60 percent of all the household wealth in America today is inherited. That's because, under U.S. tax law—which is itself largely a product of lobbying by the wealthy—the capital gains of one generation are wiped out when those assets are transferred to the next, and the estate tax is so tiny that only 0.2 percent of estates were subject to it in 2017. America is creating a new aristocracy of people who have never worked a day in their lives.

We could abolish billionaires by changing the way the system is organized. This doesn't mean confiscating the wealth and assets of the super-rich. It does mean getting rid of monopolies, stopping the use of insider information, preventing the rich from buying off politicians, and making it harder for the super-rich to avoid paying taxes—in other words, creating a system in which economic gains are shared more widely. Entrepreneurs like Jeff Bezos would be just as motivated to come up with dazzling innovations if he received $100 million, or even $50 million. But the current cost to our democracy of billionaires with enough wealth and power to change the system for their own benefit is incalculable.

. . .

The standard explanation for widening inequality is that globalization and technological change have made most Americans less competitive because the tasks we used to do can now be done more cheaply by lower-paid workers abroad or by computer-driven machines. According to this view, wages for most have stagnated because workers are worth less than they were before new technologies and globalization made many of their old jobs redundant. American workers therefore have to settle for lower wages and less security. If they want better jobs, they need more education and better skills. So hath the market decreed.

This is rubbish. No other developed nation has nearly the degree of inequality found in the United States, even though all have been exposed to the same forces of globalization and technological change. Nor can this standard explanation account for why the compensation of top corporate executives has soared from an average of 20 times that of the typical worker fifty years ago to more than 300 times today, or why the denizens of Wall Street, who in the 1950s and 1960s earned comparatively modest sums, are now paid tens of millions of dollars annually. They are hardly worth that much more now than they were worth then. American incomes and wealth have uniquely diverged over the last forty years because of the changes in the American system I have outlined. Large corporations and Wall Street have possessed the wealth and power to change the rules of the game to increase their share of the pie while reducing the share going to most Americans. CEOs have done everything possible to prevent the wages of most workers from rising in tandem with productivity gains, so that more of the gains go instead toward corporate profits, and from there mainly into the pockets of top executives, major investors, and shareholders.

Workers worried about keeping their jobs have been forced to accept this transformation without fully understanding its political roots. Public policies that emerged during the New Deal and World War II had placed most economic risks squarely on large corporations through strong unions, antitrust enforcement, and laws compensating workers for injuries, providing forty-hour workweeks with time-and-a-half for overtime, unemployment insurance, Social Security, and employer-provided health benefits (wartime price controls encouraged such tax-free benefits as substitutes for wage increases). But in the wake of the junk-bond and takeover mania of the 1980s, economic risks were shifted to workers. Corporate executives did whatever they could to reduce payrolls—outsource abroad, bust unions, install labor-replacing technologies, and utilize part-time and contract workers. New laws and regulations smoothed this transformation. Safety nets were shredded. Monopolies grew. Many labor protections disappeared. Wall Street took over.

As a result, economic insecurity has become baked into employment. Full-time workers who put in decades with a company can now find themselves without a job overnight—with no severance pay, no help finding another job, and no health insurance. Even before the crash of 2008, the Panel Study of Income Dynamics at the University of Michigan found that over any given two-year stretch in the two preceding decades, about half of all families experienced some decline in income. Today, nearly one out of every five working Americans is in a part-time job. Many are consultants, freelancers, and independent contractors. Eighty percent of Americans are living paycheck to paycheck. Employment benefits have shriveled. The portion of workers with any pension connected to their job has fallen from just over half in 1979 to under 35 percent today.

Fifty years ago, when General Motors was the largest employer in America, the typical GM worker earned $40 an hour in today's dollars. Now, America's largest employer is Walmart, and the typical entry-level Walmart worker earns $11 an hour. This isn't because the typical GM employee a half century ago was worth four times what the typical Walmart employee is now worth. The GM worker wasn't better educated or better motivated than today's Walmart worker. The real difference is GM workers a half century ago had a strong union with enough bargaining power to get a substantial share of company profits for its members. Because more than a third of workers across America belonged to a labor union, the bargains those unions struck with employers raised the wages and benefits of non-unionized workers as well. Non-union firms knew they would be unionized if they did not come close to matching the union contracts.

Today's 1.5 million Walmart workers don't have a union to negotiate a better deal for them. Because only 6.4 percent of today's private-sector workers are unionized, most employers do not have to match union contracts—which puts unionized firms at a competitive disadvantage. As I've noted, public policies have enabled and encouraged this systemic change. More states have adopted so-called right-to-work laws. The National Labor Relations Board, understaffed and overburdened, has barely enforced collective bargaining. The result has been a race to the bottom. Given these changes in the system, it's not surprising that corporate profits have increased as a portion of the total economy while wages have declined. Those whose income derives directly or indirectly from profits—corporate executives, Wall Street traders, and shareholders—have done exceedingly well. Those dependent on wages have not.

The underlying problem is not that most Americans are worth less than they had been or that they have been living beyond their means. Nor is it that they lack enough education to be sufficiently productive. The basic problem is the system itself has become tilted ever more in the direction of moneyed interests that have exerted disproportionate influence over it, while average workers have steadily lost bargaining leverage—both economic and political—to receive as large a portion of the economy's gains as they commanded in the first three decades after World War II. As a result, their means have not kept up with what the economy could otherwise provide them. To attribute this to the impersonal workings of the free market is to disregard the power of large corporations and the financial sector, which have received a steadily larger share of economic gains as a result of that power. As their gains have continued to accumulate, so has their power to accumulate even more.

The answer to this conundrum is not found in economics. It is found in politics, and it is rooted in power. The systemic changes have been reinforcing and cumulative. As more of the nation's income flows to large corporations and Wall Street and to those whose earnings and wealth derive directly from them, their political influence over the rules of the market increases, which in turn enlarges their share of total income. The more dependent politicians become on these financial favors, the greater their willingness to reorganize the system to the benefit of these moneyed interests. The weaker unions and other traditional sources of countervailing power become, the smaller their political influence over the system, which causes the playing field to tilt even further against average workers and the poor.

Ultimately, these trends in America, as elsewhere, can be reversed only if the vast majority, whose incomes have stagnated and whose wealth has failed to increase, join together to demand fundamental change. The most important political competition over the next decades will not be between the right and left or between Republicans and Democrats. It will be between a majority of Americans who have been losing ground and an economic elite that refuses to recognize or respond to the majority's growing distress.

PART III

Overcoming Oligarchy

CHAPTER 12

The Furies

IN THE FALL OF 2015, I visited Michigan, Wisconsin, Ohio, Pennsylvania, Kentucky, Missouri, and North Carolina. I was doing research on the changing nature of work in America. During my visits I spoke with many of the same people I had met twenty years before when I was secretary of labor, as well as with some of their grown children. I asked them about their jobs, their views about the economy, and their thoughts on a variety of public issues. What I was really seeking was their sense of the system as a whole and how they were faring in it.

What I heard surprised me. Twenty years before, they said they'd been working hard and were frustrated they weren't doing better. Now they were angry—angry at their employers, the government, Wall Street; angry that they hadn't been able to save for their retirement; angry that their children weren't doing any better than they did at their age. They were angry at those at the top who they felt had rigged the system for their own benefit. Several of them had lost jobs, savings, or homes in the Great Recession following the financial crisis. By the time I spoke with them, most were back in jobs, but the jobs paid no more than they had two decades before in terms of purchasing power.

I heard the term "rigged system" so often that I began asking people what they meant by it. They spoke about the bailout of Wall Street, political payoffs, insider deals, CEO pay, and "crony capitalism." These complaints came from people who identified themselves as Republicans, Democrats, and Independents. A few had joined the Tea Party. A few others had briefly been involved in the Occupy movement. Most of them didn't consider themselves political. They were white, black, and Latino, from union households and non-union. The only characteristic they had in common apart from the states and regions where I found them was their position on the income ladder. All were middle class and below.

As I've noted, in 1964 almost two-thirds of Americans believed that government was run for the benefit of all the people; by 2013, almost 80 percent believed the opposite—that government was run by and for a few big interests. The erosion in public trust was particularly steep in the wake of the Wall Street bailout and the Great Recession. In 2006, 59 percent of Americans thought government corruption was widespread; by 2013, 79 percent did. In Rasmussen polls undertaken in the fall of 2014, 66 percent believed most members of Congress didn't care what their constituents thought, and 51 percent said that even their own representative didn't care what they thought.

The people I spoke with no longer felt they had a fair chance to make it. They were sure the game was rigged against them. Here again, national polls told much the same story. In 2001, a Gallup poll found that 77 percent of Americans were satisfied with opportunities to get ahead by working hard, and only 22 percent were dissatisfied. By 2014, only 54 percent were satisfied and 45 percent were dissatisfied. According to the Pew Research Center, the percentage of Americans who feel most people who want to get ahead can do so through hard work dropped by 13 points between 2000 and 2015.

With the 2016 political primaries looming, I asked people which candidates they found most attractive. At that time, the leaders of the Democratic Party favored Hillary Clinton to be their candidate, and the leaders of the Republican Party favored Jeb Bush to be theirs. Yet no one I spoke with mentioned either Clinton or Bush. They talked about Bernie Sanders and Donald Trump. When I asked why, they said Sanders or Trump would "shake things up" or "make the system work again" or "stop the corruption" or "end the rigging."

In the following year, Sanders—a seventy-four-year-old Jew from Vermont who described himself as a democratic socialist and who wasn't even a Democrat until the 2016 presidential primary—came within a whisker of beating Hillary Clinton in the Iowa caucus, routed her in the New Hampshire primary, garnered more than 47 percent of the caucus-goers in Nevada, and ended up with 46 percent of the pledged delegates from

Democratic primaries and caucuses. Trump—a sixty-nine-year-old egomaniacal billionaire reality-TV star who had never held elective office or had anything to do with the Republican Party and who lied compulsively about almost everything—won the Republican primaries and then went on to beat Clinton, one of the most experienced and well-connected politicians in modern America (though he didn't win the popular vote, and he had some help from the Kremlin).

Something very big had happened, and it wasn't due to Sanders's magnetism or Trump's likability. It was a rebellion against the establishment. Hillary Clinton and Jeb Bush had all the advantages—deep bases of funders, well-established networks of political insiders, experienced political advisers, all the name recognition you could want—but neither of them could credibly convince voters they weren't part of the system. For decades the Clintons had built their family political enterprise on contributions from the global ultra-rich. Between their campaigns and their foundations, the couple had raised, according to *The Washington Post,* $3 billion. The financial sector forked over $21 million to Clinton's campaign, making it the largest source of her donations. Trump made the most of her establishment connections. He posed as an anti-establishment populist. It would prove to be one of the biggest cons in modern American history.

The standard economic indicators don't reflect the economic insecurity most Americans continue to feel, nor the seeming arbitrariness and unfairness they continue to experience. The indicators don't show the linkages many Americans still see between wealth and power, crony capitalism, stagnant real wages, soaring CEO pay, their own loss of status, and a billionaire class that has turned our democracy into an oligarchy. The standard measures don't show what most Americans have caught on to, how wealth has translated into political power to rig the system with bank bailouts, corporate subsidies, special tax loopholes, shrunken unions, and increasing monopoly power, all of which have further pushed down wages and pulled up profits.

Much of the political establishment still denies what has occurred. They prefer to attribute Trump's rise solely to racism. Racism did play a part. But to understand why racism (and its first cousin, xenophobia) had such a strong impact in 2016, especially on the voting of whites without college degrees, it's important to see what drove the racism. After all, racism in America dates back long before the founding of the Republic, and even modern American politicians have had few compunctions about using racism to boost their standing. Richard Nixon's "law and order" campaign on behalf of "the silent majority" was an appeal to racism. So was Ronald Reagan's condemnation of "welfare queens," and George H. W. Bush's use of Willie Horton—a black convicted felon who while on a weekend furlough committed assault and rape—to whip up white fears that Bush's opponent, Michael Dukakis, the governor of Massachusetts, where Horton had been incarcerated, would release other black convicts. Racism was also behind Bill Clinton's promise to "end welfare as we know it" and to "crack down on crime." All were illustrations of what Berkeley professor Ian Haney López has called dog-whistle politics—the use of racially coded language to exploit the prejudices of white Americans.

What gave Trump's racism—as well as his hateful xenophobia, misogyny, and jingoism—particular virulence was his capacity to channel the intensifying anger of the white working class into it. It is hardly the first time in history that a demagogue has used scapegoats to deflect public attention from the real causes of their distress. The white working-class people whom sociologist Arlie Hochschild documents in her 2018 book *Strangers in Their Own Land,* who live in a Tea Party stronghold around Lake Charles, Louisiana, are not racist. Rather, they feel marginalized by flat or falling wages, rapid demographic change, and a liberal culture that mocks their faith and patriotism. The story she kept hearing from them, in one form or another, is similar to the story I kept hearing in 2015: *You are patiently standing in a long line for something called the American dream. You are white, Christian, of modest means, and getting along in years. You are male. There are people of color behind you, and in principle you wish them well. But you've waited long, worked hard, and the line is barely moving. Then you see people cutting in line ahead of you. Who are these interlopers? Some are black, others immigrants, refugees. They get affirmative action, sympathy, and welfare—checks for the listless and idle. The government wants you to feel sorry for them. The liberal media mocks you as racist or homophobic. Everywhere you look, you feel betrayed.*

While Hochschild finds that "race is an essential part of this story," the other essential parts are feelings of declining social status and betrayal. These have nothing to do with people of color. None of the people Hochschild meets are directly hurt by competition from blacks, Latinos, or immigrants. The root cause of their distress is unchecked corporate power that has squeezed all people of modest means. The residents of the community understand this. Harold Areno, a seventy-seven-year-old Cajun man from Bayou d'Inde, Louisiana, tells Hochschild:

> The state always seems to come down on the *little* guy. Take this bayou. If your motorboat leaks a little gas into the water, the warden'll write you up. But if *companies* leak thousands of gallons of it and kill all the life here? The state lets them go. If you shoot an endangered brown pelican, they'll put you in jail. But if a company kills the brown pelican by poisoning the fish he eats? They let it go. I think they *over-regulate* the *bottom* because it's *harder* to regulate the *top*.

In 2016 Trump galvanized millions of blue-collar voters living in communities that never recovered from the tidal wave of factory closings. He understood what resonated with these voters: He promised to bring back jobs, revive manufacturing, and get tough on trade and immigration. "We can't continue to allow China to rape our country, and that's what they're doing," he said at one rally. "In five, ten years from now, you're going to have a workers' party. A party of people that haven't had a real wage increase in eighteen years, that are angry." Speaking at a factory in Pennsylvania in June 2016, he decried politicians and financiers who had betrayed Americans by "taking away from the people their means of making a living and supporting their families."

Worries about free trade used to be confined to the political left. But by 2016, according to the Pew Research Center, people who said free-trade deals were bad for America were more likely to be Republican. The problem wasn't trade itself. It was a political-economic system that had failed to cushion working people against trade's downsides or to share trade's upsides—in other words, a system that was rigged against them. Big money was at the root of the rigging. This was the premise of Sanders's 2016 campaign. It was also central to Trump's appeal ("I'm so rich I can't be bought off"), although once elected he delivered everything big money wanted. A 2016 Economist/YouGov poll found that 80 percent of GOP primary voters who preferred Donald Trump as the nominee listed money in politics as an important issue. According to a Bloomberg Politics poll, a similar percentage of Republicans were opposed to the Supreme Court's 2010 *Citizens United v. FEC* decision. Getting big money out of politics has become increasingly important to voters in both major parties. A June 2016 *New York Times/CBS News* poll showed that 84 percent of Democrats and 81 percent of Republicans wanted to fundamentally change or completely rebuild our campaign finance system. A January 2016 *Des Moines Register* poll of likely Iowa caucus-goers found 91 percent of Republicans and 94 percent of Democrats unsatisfied or "mad as hell" about money in politics.

Trump also used explicitly racial and gendered rhetoric in 2016. But to conclude from this that racism and xenophobia *caused* Trump's success misses the bigger picture. To quote three academics at the University of Massachusetts, Amherst, who did a detailed study of Trump voters, "In a campaign that was marked by exceptionally explicit rhetoric on race and gender, it is perhaps unsurprising to find that voters' attitudes on race and sex were so strongly associated with their vote choices." More to the point, blue-collar workers didn't see Hillary Clinton as their champion. As political analyst Ruy Teixeira and his coauthors put it in *The American Prospect,* "The Democrats allowed themselves to become the party of the status quo—a status quo perceived to be elitist, exclusionary, and disconnected from the entire range of working-class concerns, but particularly from those voters in white working-class areas. Rightly or wrongly, Hillary Clinton's campaign exemplified a professional-class status quo that failed to rally enough working-class voters of color and failed to blunt the drift of white working-class voters to Republicans." In 2016, Bernie Sanders did far better than Clinton with blue-collar voters. He did this by attacking trade agreements, Wall Street greed, income inequality, and big money in politics.

In other words, racism and xenophobia were proximate causes of Trump's 2016 victory, and they continue to contribute to his support. But racism was not, and is not, the underlying cause. However much the oligarchy may want Americans to believe that racism was responsible for Trump, in fact it was anti-establishment fury.

Democrats had occupied the White House for sixteen of the twenty-four years before Trump's election, and in that time they scored some important victories for working families—the Affordable Care Act, an expanded Earned Income Tax Credit, and the Family and Medical Leave Act, for example. I take pride in being part of a Democratic administration during that time. But Democrats did nothing to change the vicious cycle of wealth and power that had rigged the economy for the benefit of those at the top and undermined the working class. In some respects, Democrats were complicit in it. As Democratic pollster Stanley Greenberg concluded after the 2016 election, "Democrats don't have a 'white working-class' problem. They have a 'working class problem' which progressives have been reluctant to address honestly or boldly. The fact is that Democrats have lost support with *all* working-class voters across the electorate."

In the first two years of Bill Clinton's and Barack Obama's administrations, Democrats controlled both houses of Congress in addition to the presidency. Yet Clinton and Obama ardently pushed for free-trade agreements without providing millions of blue-collar workers who consequently lost their jobs any means of getting new ones that paid at least as well. Clinton pushed for NAFTA and for China joining the World Trade Organization, and embraced a balanced budget. Obama sought to restore the confidence of investors in financial markets instead of completely overhauling the banking system.

Both allowed antitrust enforcement to ossify, enabling large corporations to grow far larger and major industries to become more concentrated. Both stood by as corporations hammered trade unions, the backbone of the white working class. They failed to reform labor laws to allow workers to form unions with a simple up-or-down majority vote, or even to impose meaningful penalties on companies that violated labor protections. Clinton deregulated Wall Street before the crash; Obama allowed the Street to water down attempts to re-regulate it after the crash. Obama protected Wall Street from the consequences of the Street's gambling addiction through a giant taxpayer-funded bailout, but he allowed millions of underwater homeowners to drown. Both Clinton and Obama turned their backs on campaign finance reform. In 2008, Obama was the first presidential nominee since Richard Nixon to reject public financing in his primary and general election campaigns, and he never followed up on his reelection campaign promise to pursue a constitutional amendment overturning *Citizens United v. FEC*, the 2010 Supreme Court opinion opening wider the floodgates to big money in politics.

Why haven't Democrats fought harder to reverse the power shift? Although Clinton and Obama faced increasingly hostile Republican congresses, they could have rallied the working class and built a coalition to grab back power from the emerging oligarchy. Yet they chose not to. Why not? My answer is not just hypothetical, because I directly witnessed much of it: It was because Clinton, Obama, and most congressional Democrats sought the votes of the suburban swing voters—so-called soccer moms in the 1990s and affluent politically independent professionals in the 2000s—who supposedly determine electoral outcomes, and turned their backs on the working class. They also drank from the same campaign funding trough as the Republicans—big corporations, Wall Street, and the very wealthy. "Business has to deal with us whether they like it or not, because we're the majority," crowed Democratic representative Tony Coelho, head of the Democratic Congressional Campaign Committee in the 1980s, when Democrats assumed they'd continue to run the House for years. Coelho's Democrats soon achieved a rough parity with Republicans in contributions from corporate and Wall Street campaign coffers, but the deal proved to be a Faustian bargain: Democrats became financially dependent on big corporations and the Street.

Nothing in politics is ever final. Democrats could still win back the working class by putting together a huge coalition of the working class, middle class, and poor, of whites, blacks, and Latinos, of everyone who has been shafted by the shift in wealth and power to the top. This would give Democrats the political clout to get systemic reform, rather than merely enact palliative measures that paper over the increasing concentration of wealth and power in America. To do this, Democrats would have to stop obsessing over upper-income suburban swing voters and end their financial dependence on big corporations, Wall Street, and the wealthy. They would have to come down squarely on the side of democracy and against oligarchy. They would have to break with Democrats like Jamie Dimon.

Decades ago, a general election was like a competition between two hot-dog vendors on a long boardwalk extending from the right to the left. Each had to move to the middle to maximize sales. If one strayed too far left or too far right, the other would move beside him and take all sales from the rest of the boardwalk. But this view of American politics is outdated. Nowadays, it's the boardwalk versus the private jets on their way to the Hamptons. Forget left versus right. It's democracy or oligarchy. The most powerful force in American politics today is anti-establishment fury at a rigged system. There are no longer moderates. There's no longer a center. There's either authoritarian populism (Trump) or democratic populism (represented in 2016 by Bernie's "political revolution"). As Rahm Emanuel told *The New York Times* in July 2019, "This is really the crackup. Usually fights are Democrats versus Republicans, one end of Pennsylvania Avenue versus the other, or the left versus the right. Today's squabbles are internal between the establishment versus the people that are storming the barricades."

Democrats cannot defeat authoritarian populism without an agenda of radical democratic reform, a palpable anti-establishment movement. Trump harnessed the frustrations of working-class America. Even though he was a smokescreen for the emerging oligarchy—giving the oligarchy all it wanted in terms of tax cuts, regulatory rollbacks, and more wealth and power—he convinced much of the working class that he represented them. Unless Democrats stand squarely on the side of democracy against oligarchy, much of America will continue to believe him or any future politician who imitates Trump's authoritarian demagoguery.

CHAPTER 13

How Oligarchies Retain Power

HISTORY SHOWS that oligarchies cannot hold on to power forever. Oligarchies are inherently unstable. This was as true in ancient Rome as it was in America's antebellum South, where fewer than four thousand families owned about a quarter of America's capital in the form of enslaved human beings. For a time, oligarchies maintain themselves through sheer brute force. They have a monopoly on militias and weapons. But when a vast majority of people come to view an oligarchy as illegitimate and an obstacle to its own well-being, oligarchies become vulnerable to subversion, social unrest, terrorism, wars, and revolutions.

This is why oligarchies depend on ways other than brute force to hold power. The three most common are: (1) systems of belief—religions, dogmas, and ideologies—intended to convince most people of the righteousness of the oligarchy's claim to power; (2) bribes to the most influential people to gain their support and thereby legitimize the oligarchy; and (3) manufactured threats—supposed foreign enemies or "enemies within," as well as immigrants and minority populations—to divert attention from the oligarchy so the diverse elements within the majority won't join together against it.

Today's American oligarchy deploys all three.

Among the oldest methods to maintain control are belief systems that portray wealth and power in the hands of a few as natural and inevitable. King James I of England and France's Louis XIV, among other monarchs, asserted that kings received their authority from God and were therefore not accountable to their earthly subjects. The doctrine of divine right of kings ended with England's Glorious Revolution in the seventeenth century and the American and French revolutions in the eighteenth.

The modern equivalent of the divine right of kings might be termed "market fundamentalism," a creed that has been promoted by the American oligarchy with no less zeal than the old aristocracy advanced divine right. It holds that if the free market has caused a few at the top to aggregate vast wealth and power, the result must be right and good because it is natural and inevitable. One of market fundamentalism's founders was the philosopher Ayn Rand. Former Fed chair Alan Greenspan was a follower of Rand, and, as we've seen, his doctrinaire views almost sank the American economy. Today's oligarchs are not as rigidly doctrinaire, but they still regard the economy as a holy grail.

As I've said, the oligarchy wants Americans to view the system as a neutral meritocracy in which anyone can make it with enough guts, gumption, and hard work. The standard platitudes of market fundamentalism are that people "pull themselves up by their bootstraps" and that America is a nation of "self-made men" (and women), both of which translate into a moral code: People deserve whatever they earn in the market. Income and wealth are measures of worth. If you amass a billion dollars, then you must deserve it because that's what the market awarded you. If you barely scrape by, then you have only yourself to blame. It is assumed that the system, and how power is allocated within it, plays no role whatsoever.

Of course, the oligarchy doesn't want Americans to see its mounting wealth as the engorged winnings of a game whose rules it has decided on. It wants everyone to believe the oligarchy deserves what it has accumulated, even as it denies much of the rest of society the opportunities it enjoys. As the theologian Reinhold Niebuhr has written, "The most common form of hypocrisy among the privileged classes is to assume that their privileges are the just payments with which society rewards specially useful or meritorious functions," while accusing the underprivileged of "lacking what they have been denied the right to acquire."

The truth is that in America today your life chances depend largely on where your parents fit in the system—how much they earn, how much education they have, who they know.

The phrase "pulling yourself up by the bootstraps" dates back to an eighteenth-century fairy tale, a metaphor for an impossible feat of strength. In fact, it's more difficult for poor and working-class kids in America to rise economically through their working careers than it is for poor and working-class kids to rise in any other advanced nation. Over 40 percent of American children born into poor families will be poor as adults. Roughly the same share of children who are born into the richest fifth of families will remain in the richest fifth as adults.

Consider the intensifying competition to get into elite colleges, largely because of potentially huge incomes awaiting their graduates. According to data from the Department of Education, ten years after starting college, the highest-earning 10 percent of graduates from all universities have a median salary of $68,000. The top 10 percent from the ten most prestigious universities are raking in $220,000. In 2019, the Justice Department indicted dozens of wealthy parents for using bribery and fraud to get their children admitted to elite colleges. Yet the real scandal is not bribery by a few wealthy parents but how commonplace it has become for almost all wealthy parents to shell out big bucks for essay tutors, testing tutors, admissions counselors, and "enrichment" courses designed to get their kids into the college of their choice.

Elite colleges are doing their part to accelerate the trend. At a time when the courts have all but ended affirmative action for black children seeking college admission, high-end universities provide preferential admission to the children of wealthy alumni—legacies, as they're delicately called. Some prestigious colleges have even been known to make quiet deals with wealthy non-alums—admission for their kids with the expectation of a large donation to follow. Jared Kushner's father reportedly pledged $2.5 million to Harvard just as Jared was applying. The young man gained admission despite rather mediocre grades.

The most brazen affirmative-action program for children of the wealthy is the preference baked into elite admissions for graduates from private prep schools. While only 2.2 percent of American students graduate from nonsectarian private high schools, preppies account for 26 percent of students at Harvard and 28 percent of students at Princeton. All told, about 40 percent of the children of the richest 0.1 percent of American families now attend an Ivy League or other elite university. At some upscale campuses—including Dartmouth, Princeton, Yale, Penn, and Brown—more students now come from the richest 1 percent of American families than from the bottom 60 percent put together. By contrast, less than one-half of 1 percent of children from the bottom fifth of American families attend an elite college. Fewer than half attend any college at all.

A worse scandal is K–12 education, where geographic segregation by income is leaving poor school districts—partly reliant on local property taxes, which don't generate much revenue—with fewer resources per pupil than richer districts. Race is clearly involved. School districts that are predominantly white get $23 billion more funding each year than districts that serve predominantly students of color. When it comes to early childhood education—which experts agree is vital to the future life chances of the very young—the gap has become a chasm. Wealthy parents spare no expense stimulating infant and toddler brains with happy human interactions through words, music, poetry, games, and art. Yet all too often the offspring of poorer parents have little to do other than sit long hours in front of a television.

As I have noted, we now have an education system in which the oligarchy can effectively buy college admission for its children, a political system in which the oligarchy can buy Congress, a health-care system in which it can buy care others can't, and a justice system in which the oligarchy can buy its way out of jail. Consider the Wall Street executives who defrauded America in the years leading up to the 2008 financial crisis, yet went unpunished. An even more flagrant example is Ethan Couch, a Texan teenager who killed four people and severely injured another while driving drunk in June 2016. Prosecutors sought a twenty-year prison sentence, but a psychologist who testified in Couch's defense argued that the teenager suffered from "affluenza," a psychological affliction said to result from growing up with wealth and privilege. Couch served a 720-day sentence. Most poor and working-class kids accused of committing a crime can't afford a high-priced attorney. They often plead guilty in exchange for a shorter sentence than they'd get had they gone to trial and been represented by an overworked public defender. This means some end up serving far more than 720 days in prison for committing no crime at all.

In September 2019, actress Felicity Huffman was sentenced to fourteen days in jail for shelling out $15,000 to rig her daughter's SAT scores so she could get into a top university. In 2011, Kelley Williams-Bolar, a single black mother living in public housing in Akron, Ohio, was charged with multiple felonies and sentenced to two five-year sentences for using her father's address to enroll her daughters in a better public school. That same year, Tanya McDowell, a homeless black mother living in Bridgeport, Connecticut, was sentenced to five years in prison for enrolling her five-year-old son in a neighboring public school.

The myth of rugged individuals making it on their own has helped mask all of this. It has allowed the oligarchy to dismantle unions, unravel safety nets, and slash taxes on itself. And it has deterred average Americans from demanding what the citizens of every other advanced country receive—paid family and medical leave, access to child care, good schools for all, affordable health care and drugs, workable transportation and communications systems, and policies that lift every family out of poverty. As long as most Americans are convinced that they alone are responsible for their fates, they won't call for basic systemic changes—making corporations responsible to all their stakeholders, breaking up monopolies, strengthening unions, and protecting the economy from financial plundering—that would empower them to receive all these things and more.

Like the divine right of kings, market fundamentalism relies on faith rather than experience. It pretends that power has nothing to do with who wins and who loses. It proselytizes beliefs that are belied by recent history—that everyone gains from boosts in productivity and efficiency even though the oligarchy has received the lion's share; that national competitiveness increases American wages even though it has mainly increased the profits of global corporations headquartered in the United States; that the stock market is the best measure of progress even though the unbridled pursuit of profits is putting our democracy under siege and threatening the very existence of life on Earth, and most of the stock market gains since the late 1980s have come out of the paychecks of workers.

Just as with the divine right of kings whose power was thought to come from God, those who embrace market fundamentalism want Americans to ignore how a powerful few have shaped the system for their own benefit. The creed doesn't acknowledge that the rules of the free market come from government officials whose jobs increasingly depend on an oligarchy that benefits from those decisions. It doesn't accept that laws are routinely violated by corporations and CEOs that treat fines as a cost of doing business. Adherents to market fundamentalism don't see the ruthless profit-seeking behind the smooth public relations con of corporate social responsibility. They reject "socialism" without acknowledging how the oligarchy has cushioned itself against downside losses and insulated itself from personal accountability. They even view climate change as a problem of costs and inefficiencies rather than what it is—an existential threat to the future of humanity. A report issued in March 2019 by Morgan Stanley tallied $650 billion in climate-related disasters over the past three years, and predicted $54 trillion in damages worldwide by 2040. "We expect the physical risks of climate change to become an increasingly important part of the investment debate for 2019," the bank's strategists dryly write.

Market fundamentalism is as self-deluding and self-perpetuating as the divine right of kings, and with much the same result. "One of man's oldest exercises in moral philosophy," observed economist John Kenneth Galbraith, "is the search for a superior moral justification for selfishness. It is an exercise which always involves a certain number of internal contradictions and even a few absurdities. The conspicuously wealthy turn up urging the character-building value of privation for the poor."

A second means of perpetuating oligarchy is bribery to protect its power and perquisites as the price for living far more comfortably than anyone other than the oligarchs. The Russian oligarchy bribes and corrupts Russian bureaucrats. The Saudis abduct and murder internal critics but buy silence from their middle class. In America, bribes are more subtle and peaceful and are perfectly legal.

The American oligarchy pays huge sums to a vast array of corporate lawyers, tax advisers, estate planners, investment bankers, money managers, private equity managers, accountants, financial advisers, management consultants, lobbyists, business strategists, economists, and marketing and public relations professionals to defend and enlarge the oligarchy's wealth and power. This is not part of their official job descriptions, of course. A few of them may even have been hired to promote "corporate social responsibility." But defending and enlarging the oligarchy's hold is what they are actually paid to do. They are the palace guard that protects the oligarchs while continuously siphoning power and resources from the bottom 90 percent.

Most of the palace guard are highly educated. Over 40 percent of Ivy League graduates end up in finance, management consulting, and corporate law. Their annual salaries are typically in the hundreds of thousands of dollars. As of 2018, it took $1.3 million of net worth to make it into the richest 10 percent, and most of the palace guard are comfortably above that threshold. They own 80 percent of the stock market, as I've said. Most reside in or around Washington, D.C., New York, and coastal California, within America's most comfortable zip codes with the best public schools and amenities, the lowest rates of crime, and the fastest-rising home prices. They are overwhelmingly white. According to the Pew Research Center, Latinos comprise 2.4 percent of the richest 10 percent; African Americans, 1.9 percent; other minorities, including Asian and multiracial individuals, 8.8 percent.

All these enablers would not want to be seen, nor do they see themselves, as defenders and promoters of the oligarchy. They don't consider themselves bought or bribed. They view themselves as professionals of the highest integrity who do excellent work and adhere to professional standards and ethical codes. The stark reality, though, is that their careers are dedicated to preserving and defending the system and to helping the oligarchy aggregate even more wealth and power. Directly or indirectly, their paychecks are drawn from the oligarchy's wealth. They know the oligarchy is consolidating ever greater wealth and power, but they will not criticize it. Their livelihood depends on it. They certainly will not seek to reduce its power.

Many of them are socially liberal. They favor diversity and inclusion, equal marriage rights for gays and lesbians, transgender bathrooms, and a woman's right to choose. They want more women, blacks, and Latinos on corporate boards, in executive suites, and as members of Congress. Most resolutely disapprove of racism, white privilege, misogyny, and xenophobia in America. They worry about the destruction of the environment. But they avoid questions of class and power like the plague. Personal issues of identity are on the table, but the *system* is not. They accept the erosion of upward mobility as long as a diverse enough group of high achievers can climb from top universities to the C-suites. They overlook the demise of democratic institutions as long as more women and blacks are elected to public office. They disregard corporate predation of the environment as long as corporations make conspicuous displays of social responsibility.

Just before the 2016 presidential election, researchers at the Harvard Business School polled students on their choice of candidate. Eighty-five percent supported Hillary Clinton, while only 3 percent backed Trump (by way of comparison, Trump got the votes of 32 percent of Massachusetts residents beyond the Harvard Business School). Harvard Business School students overwhelmingly preferred Clinton because she reflected their own undemanding blend of inclusive liberalism and keep-the-system-as-is conservativism, while Trump's racism and xenophobia offended their ethic of inclusion and diversity. It was also true that Hillary Clinton personified the system and how to succeed within it. The Harvard students had bought into that system and, by implication, had bought into the emerging oligarchy that controlled and fed off the system. To that extent, the system and the oligarchy had bought them, too.

The oligarchy also buys the support of nonprofit institutions and universities, whose inhabitants are supposed to be truth tellers but will sometimes pull their punches rather than lose funding. As more of the nation's wealth consolidates in fewer hands, nonprofits and universities have little choice but to solicit handouts from the oligarchs. Sometimes the handouts come with strings. Since its founding in 1999, the think tank New America—an important voice in policy debates—has received more than $21 million from Google, from its parent company's executive chair, Eric Schmidt, and from his family's foundation. According to *The New York Times,* one of New America's initiatives, Open Markets, had been critical of the market power of tech giants like Google. The researcher who headed that initiative posted a statement on New America's website praising the European Union's penalty against Google for monopolization. Schmidt communicated his displeasure to the think tank's president, who accused the researcher of "imperiling the institution as a whole" and shut down the Open Markets initiative.

New America isn't the only recipient of Google's largesse. Despite its avowed concern about climate change, Google has made large donations to some of the most notorious climate change deniers in Washington, including the Heartland Institute, an anti-science group that has attacked teenage activist Greta Thunberg for "climate delusion hysterics," and Heritage Action, which has alleged that the Paris climate accord is supported by "cosmopolitan elites." Presumably, Google has made these donations because such groups don't want government intruding on corporate America, especially Google.

I'm aware of a nonprofit devoted to voting rights that decided not to launch a campaign against big money in politics for fear of alienating the wealthy donors it courts, and a liberal-leaning Washington think tank that released a study on inequality that failed to mention the role big corporations and Wall Street have played in weakening the nation's labor and antitrust laws, presumably because the think tank didn't want to antagonize its corporate and Wall Street donors. I was asked to participate in an academic effort to raise money to study inequality, but when I suggested that part of the study should focus on the political power of the wealthy, I was told the topic couldn't be included because wealthy donors would find it offensive.

Major universities often shape research and courses around economic topics of interest to their biggest donors, notably avoiding any mention of the increasing power of large corporations and Wall Street. Google has quietly financed hundreds of university professors who write research papers justifying Google's market dominance. The Charles Koch Foundation has funded 350 programs at more than 250 colleges and universities across America. You can bet that funding doesn't underwrite research on inequality and environmental justice.

The oligarchy is not above bribing journalists and their news outlets, either. It wines and dines celebrity journalists in Aspen, Davos, and other upscale conclaves. It doles out high speaking fees to journalists for anodyne talks on the affairs of the day. It finances, in whole or in part, business journals, business columns, and internet-based curated news magazines. In return, the journalists and outlets report what the oligarchy wants them to report and avoid items the oligarchy prefers the public not know. The late David Koch's $23 million of donations to public television guaranteed that a documentary critical of the Kochs did not air.

The third means of perpetuating oligarchy is through diverting the attention of the bottom 90 percent from the oligarchy's increasing wealth and power toward scapegoats such as immigrants, African Americans, Latinos, and Muslims, while at the same time dividing the nation into warring cultural tribes. Americans who are angry and suspicious of one another will fight over the crumbs rather than join together against those who have run off with most of the pie.

In public, the oligarchy disapproves of racism. As I've noted, Jamie Dimon and other CEOs quit Trump's business advisory councils after Trump's reaction to the fatal confrontation in Charlottesville. Most young people who aspire to become CEOs or at least members of the palace guard, such as students at Harvard Business School, reject racism and xenophobia. But, as I've suggested, the astounding silence of the CEOs in the face of Donald Trump's continuing bigotry and their eagerness to fund his elections and those of his Republican enablers suggests another motive. They won't explicitly encourage divisiveness, but they will tolerate it. They will publicly decry racism and xenophobia, but privately, huddled with their lobbyists and government-relations advisers, they understand that a divide-and-conquer strategy gives them more room to maneuver. This is not a new strategy. A half century ago, Martin Luther King Jr. observed much the same about the old South. "The Southern aristocracy took the world and gave the poor white man Jim Crow," he said following the 1965 march from Selma to Montgomery, Alabama, "and when his wrinkled stomach cried out for the food that his empty pockets could not provide, he ate Jim Crow, a psychological bird that told him that no matter how bad off he was, at least he was a white man, better than a black man."

Trump is the best thing ever to have happened to the new American oligarchy. In addition to his tax cuts and regulatory rollbacks, he stokes divisiveness in ways that keeps the bottom 90 percent from seeing how the oligarchy has taken over the reins of government, twisted government to its benefit, and siphoned off the economy's benefits. His deal with the oligarchy has been simple: He'll stoke division and tribalism so most Americans won't see CEOs getting exorbitant pay while they're slicing the pay of average workers, won't pay attention to the giant tax cut that went to big corporations and the wealthy, and won't notice a boardroom culture that tolerates financial conflicts of interest, insider trading, and the outright bribery of public officials through unlimited campaign donations.

Trump knows how to pit native-born Americans against immigrants, the working class against the poor, whites against blacks and Latinos. He is well-versed in getting evangelicals and secularists steamed up about abortion, equal marriage rights, out-of-wedlock births, access to contraception, transgender bathrooms. He knows how to stir up fears of brown-skinned people from "shitholes" streaming across the border to murder and rape, and how to stoke anger about black athletes who don't stand for the national anthem. He's a master at fueling anxieties about so-called communists, socialists, and the "America-hating left" taking over the nation. He can make the white working class believe they've been losing good jobs and wages because of a cabal of Democrats, immigrants, and "deep state" bureaucrats. Schooled in reality television and New York City tabloids, Trump knows how to keep almost everyone stirred up: vilify, disparage, denounce, defame, and accuse the other side of conspiring against America, and do it continuously. Dominate every news cycle. Trump isn't interested in converting large numbers to a cause. His goal is cynicism, disruption, and division. That way, he and the oligarchy behind him can rig the system and then complain loudly that the system is rigged.

His arguments about "them" are completely false, of course. Undocumented workers aren't taking away the jobs of American citizens. They aren't committing more crimes. Immigrants aren't draining social services. Muslims aren't terrorists. Black athletes who protest police brutality are no less patriotic than any other Americans, nor are Democratic representatives of color. Nor is America suffering a breakdown in private morality. To the contrary, it's burdened by a breakdown in *public* morality. What Americans do in their bedrooms and with their bodies is their own business. What corporate executives and Wall Street financiers do in boardrooms and executive suites affects all of us.

CHAPTER 14

Why Democracy Will Prevail

IF STAGNANT WAGES, near-record inequality, climate change, nuclear standoffs, assault weapons and mass killings, Russian trolls, kids locked in cages at our border, and Donald Trump's presidency don't at least occasionally cause you feelings of impending doom, you're not human. But as bad as it looks right now, as despairing as you can sometimes feel, the great strength of this country is our resilience. We bounce back. We will again.

Not convinced? Come back in time with me to when I graduated college in 1968. That year, Martin Luther King Jr. and Robert F. Kennedy were assassinated. Our cities were burning. Tens of thousands of young Americans were being ordered to Vietnam to fight an unwinnable and unjust war, which ultimately claimed more than 58,000 American lives and the lives of more than 3 million Vietnamese. The nation was deeply divided. In November of that year, Richard Nixon was elected president. I recall thinking America would never recover. Somehow, though, we bounced back.

In subsequent years we enacted the Environmental Protection Act. We achieved marriage equality for gays and lesbians. We elected a black man to be president of the United States. We passed the Affordable Care Act.

Even now, it's not as bleak as it sometimes seems. In 2018, a record number of women, people of color, and LGBTQ were elected to Congress, including the first Muslim women. Eighteen states raised their minimum wages. Surprising things are happening even in traditionally conservative states. In Tennessee, a Republican legislature has enacted free community college and raised taxes for infrastructure. Nevada has expanded voting rights and gun controls. New Mexico has increased spending by 11 percent and raised its minimum wage by 60 percent. Teachers have gone on strike in Virginia, Oklahoma, West Virginia, Kentucky, and North Carolina—and won. The public sided with the teachers.

In several states, after decades of tough-on-crime policies, conservative groups have joined with liberals to reform criminal justice systems. Early childhood education and alternative energy promotion have also expanded nationwide, largely on a bipartisan basis. In 2018, South Carolina passed a law giving pregnant workers and new mothers more protections in the workplace. The law emerged from an unlikely coalition— supporters of abortion rights and religious groups that oppose them. A similar alliance in Kentucky enacted laws requiring that employers provide reasonable accommodations for pregnant workers and new mothers.

The arc of American history reveals an unmistakable pattern. Whenever privilege and power conspire to pull us backward, we eventually rally and move forward. Sometimes it takes an economic shock like the bursting of a giant speculative bubble; sometimes we just reach a tipping point where the frustrations of average Americans turn into action. Look at the progressive reforms between 1900 and 1916; the New Deal of the 1930s; the civil rights struggle of the 1950s and 1960s; the widening opportunities for women, minorities, people with disabilities, and gays, starting in the 1960s and continuing, in fits and starts, to the present day; and the environmental reforms of the 1970s.

Now, come forward in time with me. Look at the startling diversity of younger Americans. The majority of Americans now under eighteen years old are ethnically Latino, Asian or Pacific Islander, African American, or bi- or multiracial. In ten years, it's estimated that most Americans under thirty will be. Three decades from now, most of America will be. That diversity will be a huge strength. It means, I hope, we will be more tolerant, less racist, less xenophobic.

Our young people are also determined to make America better. They voted in record numbers in the 2018 midterms. I've been teaching for almost forty years, and I've never taught a generation of students as dedicated to public service, as committed to improving the nation and the world, as is the generation I'm now teaching. That's another sign of our future strength.

Meanwhile, the majority of college students today are women, which means that in future years even more women will be in leadership positions—in science, politics, education, nonprofits, and corporate suites. That will also be a great boon to America.

To state it another way, there is ample reason for hope. But hope is not enough. In order for real change to occur, the locus of power in the system will have to change.

We don't lack for policy ideas—Medicare for All, a Green New Deal, better schools and opportunities for all our children, a tax on great wealth to pay for all this, and many others. Yet even the best policy ideas are meaningless without the power to implement them. Some policy victories can still be achieved within the system, and policy advocates must continue their hard work. But as wealth and power concentrate at the top, systemic change is becoming more urgent. Policy advocates have no hope of long-term success without the efforts of change insurgents who mobilize the public to protect democracy itself, and shift power from the oligarchy to the majority. It is not possible to respond to the nation's or the world's urgent problems without a fully functioning democracy, and democracy cannot be achieved unless power is reallocated.

This will not happen automatically or easily. A just society will not emerge simply because a few green shoots are visible or because demographics are on our side. History shows that whenever we have stalled or slipped, the nation's forward movement has depended on the active engagement and commitment of vast numbers of Americans who are morally outraged by how far our economy and our democracy have strayed from our ideal and are committed to move beyond outrage to real reform. Your outrage and your commitment are needed once again. Millions will need to be organized and energized, not just for a particular election but for an ongoing movement, not just for a particular policy but to reclaim democracy so an abundance of good policies are possible. Americans must understand the system, where the status quo is most entrenched, and where change is most readily possible. They must also comprehend the corrosive relationship between great wealth and great power. If wealth continues to concentrate at the top, it will be impossible to contain the corrupting influence of big money. As Justice Louis D. Brandeis once said, "We can have democracy in this country or we can have great wealth concentrated in the hands of a few, but we can't have both."

As a kid I was always a head shorter than other boys, which meant I was bullied—mocked, threatened, sometimes assaulted. Childhood bullying has been going on forever. Over the last four decades, America has developed a culture of bullying that's fiercer than anything I experienced as a kid. Wealthier Americans bully poorer Americans, CEOs bully their workers, people with privilege and pedigree bully those without, whites bully people of color, men bully women, people born in America bully new arrivals. Sometimes the bullying involves physical violence, but more often it entails intimidation, displays of dominance, demands for submission, or arbitrary decisions over the lives of those who feel they have no choice but to accept them. At its core, bullying is about power—typically the power of those who are rich, white, privileged, or male, or all of the above, to threaten and intimidate those who are not.

At some point, those who are bullied gain the courage to fight back. I remember the exact day I did, when I had had enough. I was ten years old. One morning when I was waiting for the school bus, a local bully started shaking me down. He wanted my lunch box and the change in my pocket. He began threatening me physically, as he had done several times before. I felt the rage well up inside me. I put down my lunch box and let him have it.

Trump is America's bully-in-chief. He exemplifies those who use their wealth to gain power and celebrity, harass or abuse women and get away with it, lie and violate the law with impunity, and rage against anyone who calls them on their bullying. Trump became president by exploiting the anger of millions of white working-class Americans who for decades have been economically bullied by corporate executives and Wall Street. Even as profits have ballooned and executive pay has gone into the stratosphere, workers have been hammered. Their pay has gone nowhere, their benefits have shrunk, their jobs are less secure, their health has worsened. Trump used this anger to build his political base, channeling people's frustrations and anxieties into racism and nativism. He has encouraged Americans who have been bullied to feel more powerful by bullying people with even less power—poor blacks, Latinos, immigrants, Muslims, families seeking asylum.

This bullying game has been played repeatedly in history by self-described strongmen who pretend to be tribunes of the oppressed by scapegoating the truly powerless. Trump is no tribune of the people. He and his enablers, mostly but not exclusively in the Republican Party, work for the oligarchs— cutting their taxes, eliminating regulations, allowing some of them to profit off public lands and coastal waters, and slashing public services.

Eventually those who are bullied will gain the courage to fight back and reclaim economic and political power. Perhaps a new virtuous cycle will begin inside what I've termed the professional palace guard, those who are comfortably within the top 10 percent. It will emerge among the legions of corporate lawyers, high-priced accountants, management consultants, mid-level executives, public relations specialists, nonprofit heads, and journalists who have protected the oligarchy or been bribed into silence. Some will decide they can no longer make moral meaning out of their lives unless they cease taking those bribes. They will reject the obscenity of ever more concentrated wealth and power. They will commit to reversing the vicious cycle even if that means living less comfortably.

In addition, some who are now typically on the right of the old political spectrum—family businesses, farmers, individual contractors, lone entrepreneurs, and inhabitants of smaller communities—will discover they have much in common with women, minorities, and urban professionals. All are paying more for pharmaceuticals, broadband connections, food, credit card debt, and health insurance than they would if the rules of the market weren't shaped by big corporations. Many small businesses and entrepreneurs are being squeezed by monopolies, franchisees are trapped in contracts that siphon off most of their profits, creditors and contractors are stonewalled by big corporations that won't pay their bills. If they see their common interests, they will ally themselves and come to see market fundamentalism for what it is—a religion that idolizes the free market while masking those with power over the rules of the game.

They will reject the talismans of growth and efficiency unless the benefits of growth and efficiency are broadly shared and their costs and burdens no longer fall downward on them. They will stop defining "national competitiveness" as the profitability of large global corporations and see it as the productivity of the American people—who in order to be productive require good education and health care and a world-class infrastructure. They'll recognize corporate social responsibility as nothing more than a thinly veiled public relations con. There can be no responsibility without laws that force corporations to sacrifice some shareholder gains for the benefit of workers, communities, and society. And they'll understand that laws themselves are meaningless if large corporations can continue to violate them whenever the resulting fines are lower than the benefits derived from their illegality.

They'll see that the current American system is not a meritocracy where ability and hard work are rewarded but a cruel sham dominated by wealth and privilege. They'll understand that politics is no longer a series of electoral contests between Democrats and Republicans. They'll see the real contest as between a small minority who have gained power over the system and the vast majority who have little or none.

Class consciousness alone, however, will not overcome deep divisions of culture, history, and identity that have cleaved us apart. It is difficult to imagine the bottom 90 percent joining together in a multiracial, multiethnic coalition of working-class, poor, and middle-class Americans at a time when white voters without college degrees are repeatedly told that the country has been taken over by undocumented immigrants, Latinos, African Americans, and a "deep state" of coastal liberals, intelligence agencies, and the mainstream media. Trump and other demagogues are masterful at telling big lies, and they are backed by the oligarchy's big money. It is also difficult to imagine such a coalition emerging when people of color are threatened by mass incarceration and mass deportation, and when women face new restrictions on reproductive freedom. Fear for oneself and one's family is a potent deterrent to collective action.

Creating such a coalition will therefore require something more than class consciousness. It will necessitate a common understanding of what it means to be a citizen with responsibilities for the greater good. The reason to fight oligarchy is not just to obtain a larger slice of the economic winnings; it is to make democracy function so that we can achieve all the goals we hold in common.

·   ·   ·

The major fault line in American politics is already shifting—from Democrat versus Republican to democracy versus oligarchy. Unless one or both of the two major parties in the United States moves away from the established centers of political and economic power, a new party could unite the disaffected and anti-establishment elements of both major parties and give voice to the 90 percent of Americans who have been losing ground.

This is not far-fetched. As recently as July 2004, only 27 percent of Americans called themselves Independent in Gallup polling. Today, 46 percent do. In 2003, 56 percent of Americans interviewed by Gallup said the two political parties did an adequate job. By 2018, 57 percent said a third major party was needed. Younger Americans are even more persuaded. More than 70 percent in an NBC/GenForward poll in 2017 said they wanted a third party. As Representative Justin Amash of Michigan, who supported impeaching Trump, observed when he left the Republican Party on July 4, 2019, "The two-party system has evolved into an existential threat to American principles and institutions." The growing desire for a third party doesn't mean one will become a dominant force in American politics, though. The American political system discourages strong third parties through winner-take-all rules that squeeze out insurgents, which is why third parties tend to drain off votes from the dominant party closest to them in ideology or voter preference.

Some believe we elect politicians so the rest of us don't have to be actively engaged in politics. Politics is *their* job. This view is plainly wrong. Citizenship entails more than voting on election days. It requires ongoing engagement—knowing what needs to be done, getting the facts and understanding the arguments, and then making enough of a ruckus, and organizing and mobilizing others to join you, to do what needs to be done. Most of us don't practice active citizenship because we tell ourselves we're too busy for it. Yet we do other things that are arguably less important—swimming or crossword puzzles or cards or cooking, for example. Of course we have the time. The real reason most of us don't practice citizenship is we don't know how, and we fear we cannot be effective.

I hope I've convinced you that you must at least try. Few things we possess and will hand on to our children and grandchildren are more precious than our democracy. Few things we believe in will affect the lives of our children and grandchildren more fundamentally than our commitment to a fair and just society. That precious possession and that fundamental ideal are both gravely endangered. They can be protected only by engaged citizens who know the truth and are willing to fight to reclaim our democracy.

The challenge we face is large and complex, but I do want to remind you of how resilient America has been and how well situated we are for the fight ahead. The forces of greed and hate would prefer you give up fighting for a more just society because that way they win. We have no choice but to continue the fight. The American economy cannot be sustained if the richest 10 percent continue to reap almost all the economic gains while the poorest 90 percent are left behind. American democracy cannot be maintained if the voices of the vast majority continue to be ignored. Democracy will prevail, if we fight for it.

CHAPTER 15

A Final Word to Mr. Dimon

MR. DIMON, since I have referred to you a great deal in this book, I want to devote a few final words to you. I hope you now see that the only way to do the admirable things you advocate in your public pronouncements—ensure that the needs of all our citizens are being met, lift middle-class incomes, fulfill the promise of equal opportunity, and end climate change—is to do something you have shown no interest in doing: Give up your power and get your colleagues at the Business Roundtable and other members of the American oligarchy to do the same. Then support systemic changes that ensure that no one can ever again siphon off so many of the economic gains for themselves while undermining so much of our democracy.

As I've said, we need to change corporate governance so workers and communities have a larger voice in corporate decision making. Although your Business Roundtable now appears receptive to this idea, I very much doubt you and your fellow CEOs are prepared to sacrifice share prices (as well as all your pay that's tied to those share prices) to achieve it—which is what it will require. Recall that since 1989 most of the gains in the stock market have come at the expense of workers. As I have shown, shareholder activists like Carl Icahn, along with their slightly more respectable associates in private equity, will keep it that way unless laws prevent them.

You and your colleagues also assert a commitment to "supporting the communities in which we work," but how is that supposed to happen when your corporations demand and get state and local tax abatements as a condition for remaining in those communities, or as a lure to relocate to another? As I've noted, twenty-one of the CEOs signing your statement preside over hugely profitable corporations that didn't pay a cent of federal income tax in 2018, in part due to the corporate tax cut you and they successfully lobbied for. Your bank, JPMorgan Chase, got a whopping tax cut, too. The programs you've initiated for worker training and affordable housing are commendable, but they're insignificant compared to those tax cuts. How do you expect our communities to pay for the schools, roads, clean water, and social services they need unless you and your colleagues push for higher taxes on corporations and yourselves?

If you and the other members of your Business Roundtable were serious about becoming responsible to all your stakeholders, you'd use your formidable political power to *reduce* your power relative to them. You'd seek legislation binding yourself and every other major corporation to have worker representatives on your boards of directors, mandating that workers receive a certain percentage of shares of stock, requiring that your corporations recognize a union when a majority of your workers want one, giving the communities where you operate a say before your corporations abandon them, and imposing higher corporate taxes in order to support your workers and your communities. You'd also treat the environment as your largest stakeholder and fight like hell to preserve it. None of your other stakeholders, not even your largest shareholders, will survive when the planet becomes uninhabitable.

Also, given the mammoth size of your bank and the four other huge banks on Wall Street, and the increasing size and market concentration of all the corporations that make up the Business Roundtable, you would seek to revive antitrust legislation. You and I both know huge size translates into even more bargaining clout with all other stakeholders, including politicians—which is giving you and the other behemoths the power to siphon off still more wealth from everyone else, the opposite of social responsibility. But let me warn you that gigantic size will also make you a sitting duck when the political winds shift, or when the next financial crisis occurs. Wouldn't it make more sense to support strong antitrust enforcement that would break up your bank and the other behemoths on the Street before this happens? Similarly, it would make sense to urge that the five high-tech giants be broken up, or at least that their intellectual property be made available to smaller competitors, so that their political and economic power is defused before they do even more damage and become the targets of even more public hostility than they are already attracting.

I doubt you will push to revive antitrust laws for the same reason I doubt you'll seek legislation to make corporations accountable to all their stakeholders. Both would require that you and your Business Roundtable colleagues relinquish some of your own wealth and power. Nor is it likely that you will get behind efforts to provide more protection for consumers and investors against looting and fraud by the financial sector. In fact, since the financial crisis, you have been spending much of your time and political clout trying to whittle away at what's left of financial regulations. I also don't expect you to push for laws and constitutional changes to reduce the power of big money in our political system, because that, too, would reduce your own wealth and power. You probably like the way wealth and power are currently allocated in the system because, after all, you helped create the current system.

You are not a bad man, Mr. Dimon, and I prefer to believe that you haven't been fully aware of the consequences of what you have wrought. But if you have read this book up to this point, you understand that you and the other oligarchs are America's hidden bullies. Together you have enlarged your net worth by repressing wages and pushing the companies you invest in to do so as well, and you have enlarged your political power by flooding our system with your money. You and your colleagues' capacity to bully has grown as the nation's wealth has become concentrated, as the economy has become more monopolized, and as American politics has become more engulfed in big money.

I admire some of the things you have accomplished in your career, and I did appreciate your taking the time from your busy schedule to phone me. But you are partly responsible for the system we have today, a system that almost everyone knows is not working, which most Americans see as rigged against them, which has siphoned off much of the wealth of the country for itself, invited demagogues to run for political office and pushed voters to elect them, done little to protect the planet from devastating climate change, and drained much of our democracy of its vitality. And because you are responsible for this system, I believe that you at least have a moral duty *not* to use your formidable political power to stop the movement toward a more just system.

The heat is rising. The tectonic plates are on the move. Democracy and oligarchy are crushing up against one another. If you wait too long, you are asking for even more dysfunction and resentment than already infects this land. If you and the other members of the oligarchy stand in the way, you will be complicit in wherever this leads.

If we had had more time on the phone, I would have said all this to you directly. This book will have to suffice.

Acknowledgments

This book has benefited from the insights of many people I've had the privilege to know and to work with over the years, among them Bob Edgar, Karen Hobart Flynn, John Kenneth Galbraith, Gabrielle Giffords, Tom Glynn, Arlie Russell Hochschild, Ted Kennedy, Bill Moyers, Richard Neustadt, Michael Pertschuk, Bernie Sanders, Martha Tierney, Elizabeth Warren, Paul Wellstone, Fred Wertheimer, and Tracy Weston. I am also grateful to my colleagues at the University of California, Berkeley, for fostering the intellectually courageous community that is my home, and to four decades of hardworking and eager students at Berkeley, Brandeis, and Harvard, who have taught me more than I ever taught them. Thanks are also due to Dean Henry Brady at the Goldman School of Public Policy for his help and enthusiasm, to my able assistant Aarin Walker, to Steve Silberstein and Richard Blum for valued support, and to my talented teammates at Inequality Media, including Yael Bridge, Courtney Fuller, Eddie Geller, Jacob Kornbluth, Sasha Leitman, Heather Lofthouse, Katie Milne, Kyle Parker, and Andrew Santana. Special thanks to Brad DeLong, Elizabeth Doty, John Isaacson, Ian Haney López, and Harley Shaiken for sparking several of the ideas contained herein. This book could not have been written without the help of my literary agent and friend, Rafe Sagalyn, and my gifted editor and friend, Jonathan Segal, both of whom have been at my side since the start. Finally, and in countless ways, I am indebted to my partner and wife, Perian Flaherty, whose love continues to inspire and sustain me.

A Note on Sources

This book draws on economic and political data and analyses, as well as biography, history, and political philosophy. For convenience, I have grouped the sources I found most useful into the categories below.

Data and Analyses on Widening Disparities of
Income and Wealth in the United States

Atkinson, Anthony, Thomas Piketty, and Emmanuel Saez. "Top Incomes in the Long Run of History." *Journal of Economic Literature,* 2011; series maintained in World Inequality Database, http://wid.world.

Barnichon, Regis, Christian Matthes, and Alexander Ziegenbein. "The Financial Crisis at 10: Will We Ever Recover?" Federal Reserve Bank of San Francisco, Economic Letter, August 13, 2018.

Bureau of Economic Analysis, U.S. Department of Commerce, Current Population Survey and Annual Social and Economic Supplement, various years.

Bureau of Labor Statistics of U.S. Department of Labor.

Chetty, Raj, John N. Friedman, Emmanuel Saez, Nicholas Turner, and Danny Yagan. "Mobility Report Cards: The Role of Colleges in Intergenerational Mobility." NBER, January 2017.

CNBC. "Promises, Problems on Horizon as $30 Trillion Wealth Transfer Looms." February 21, 2017.

Economic Policy Institute. "CEO Compensation Has Grown 940% Since 1978." August 14, 2019.

———. "Inequality, Exhibit A: Walmart and the Wealth of American Families." July 17, 2012.

EdBuild. "Nonwhite School Districts Get $23 Billion Less Than White Districts." EdBuild.org, February 27, 2019.

"Hours Worked." Organization for Economic Cooperation and Development, 2018.

Piketty, Thomas, Emmanuel Saez, and Gabriel Zucman. "Distributional Accounts: Methods and Estimates for the United States." *Quarterly Journal of Economics*, 2018.

Saez, Emmanuel, and Gabriel Zucman. "Wealth Inequality in the United States Since 1913: Evidence from Capitalized Income Tax Data." *Quarterly Journal of Economics*, May 2016.

Data and Analyses on the Increasing Political Influence of the Wealthiest Americans

Gilens, Martin, and Benjamin Page. "Testing Theories of American Politics: Elites, Interest Groups, and Average Citizens." *Perspectives on Politics*. American Political Science Association, March 2014.

Greenwald, Daniel, Martin Lettau, and Sydney C. Ludvigon. "How the Wealth Was Won: Factors Shares as Market Fundamentals." NBER Working Paper No. w25769, April 2019.

MacInnis, Bo, Sarah Anderson, and Jon Krosnick. "Process Approval and Democratic Legitimacy: How Americans

Want Their Elected Representatives to Decide How to Vote." *Democratic Representation,* February 2018.

Open Secrets, Center for Responsive Politics, various years.

Page, Benjamin, Larry Bartels, and Jason Seawright. "Democracy and the Political Preferences of Wealthy Americans." *Perspectives on Politics.* American Political Science Association, March 2013.

Schlozman, Kay Lehman, Sidney Verba, and Henry E. Brady. *The Unheavenly Chorus: Unequal Political Voice and the Broken Promise of American Democracy.* Princeton, NJ: Princeton University Press, 2012.

Polls and Analyses of American Public Opinion About Widening Inequality and Political Corruption

American National Election Studies, The ANES Guide to Public Opinion and Electoral Behavior, various years.

Bloomberg Poll. "Americans Want Supreme Court to Turn Off Political Spending Spigot." September 28, 2015.

The Economist/YouGov Poll. "Money in Politics." June 2–5, 2016.

Gallup. "Americans Continue to Embrace Political Independence." January 7, 2019.

———. "In U.S., 67% Dissatisfied with Income, Wealth Distribution." January 20, 2014.

———. "Majority in U.S. Still Say a Third Party Is Needed." October 26, 2018.

Iowa Poll. "Money in Politics." January 2016.

NBC/GenForward Poll. "Strong Majority Want a Third Party." November 29, 2017.

The New York Times/CBS News Poll. "Americans' Views on Money in Politics." June 2, 2015.

Pew Research Center. "Looking Ahead to 2050, Americans Are
   Pessimistic About Many Aspects of Life in U.S." March 21, 2019.
———. "Republicans, Especially Trump Supporters, See Free Trade
   Deals as Bad for U.S." March 31, 2016.
———. "10 Facts About American Workers." August 2019.
———. "Trust in Government: 1958–2015." November 23, 2015.
Rasmussen Reports. "Voters Think Congress Cheats to Get
   Reelected." September 3, 2014.

The Corporation, Finance, and Labor

Banking on Climate Change: Fossil Fuel Finance Report Card, 2019.
Business Roundtable. *Statement on the Purpose of a Corporation,*
   1997.
———. *Statement on the Purpose of a Corporation,* 2019.
Dalio, Ray. "Why and How Capitalism Needs to Be
   Reformed." April 5, 2019, https://economicprinciples.org/
   Why-and-How-Capitalism-Needs-To-Be-Reformed/.
Egan, Mark L., Gregor Matvos, and Amit Seru. "Arbitration with
   Uninformed Consumers." NBER Working Paper No. 25150,
   revised June 2019.
Financial Crisis Inquiry Commission. *Financial Crisis Inquiry
   Commission Report,* January 2011.
GE Annual Reports, 2018, 2017, 2016.
GM Annual Reports, 2018, 2017, 2016.
Greenhouse, Steven. *Beaten Down, Worked Up: The Past, Present,
   and Future of Organized Labor.* New York: Alfred A. Knopf,
   2019.
Jensen, Michael C., and William H. Meckling. "Theory of the
   Firm: Managerial Behavior, Agency Costs and Ownership
   Structure." *Journal of Financial Economics,* October 1976,
   pp. 205–360.

National Science Board. Science and Engineering Indicators, 2018, National Science Foundation, 2018.

Roosevelt, Theodore. *The New Nationalism.* 1910.

Thurm, Scott. "U.S. Firms Add Jobs, but Mostly Overseas." *Wall Street Journal,* April 27, 2012.

Politics and Partisanship

Benjamin, John. "Business Class: Inside the Strange, Uniform Politics of Today's MBA Programs—and What It Says About American Elites." *The New Republic,* May 14, 2018.

Edsell, Thomas B. "Republicans Sure Love to Hate Unions." *New York Times,* November 18, 2014.

Griffin, Robert, John Halpin, and Ruy Teixeira. "Democrats Need to Be the Party of and for Working People—of All Races." *American Prospect,* June 1, 2017.

Schaffner, Brian, Matthew MacWilliams, and Tatishe Nteta. "Understanding White Polarization in the 2016 Vote for President: The Sobering Role of Racism and Sexism." *Political Science Quarterly,* March 25, 2018.

Political Theory

Neibuhr, Reinhold. *Moral Man and Immoral Society: A Study in Ethics and Politics.* New York: Charles Scribner's Sons, 1932.

Popper, Karl, *The Open Society and Its Enemies.* 1945; Princeton, NJ: Princeton University Press, 2013.

Rawls, John. *Justice as Fairness.* 1985; Boston: Belknap Press, 2001.

Sandel, Michael. *Liberalism and the Limits of Justice.* 1982; Cambridge: Cambridge University Press, 1998.

Jamie Dimon and JPMorgan Chase

Jamie Dimon profiles and news reports drawn from *Bloomberg News, Forbes, Fortune, Business Insider, The New York Times, Vanity Fair, New York Magazine, Crain's New York Business, Wall Street Journal, Washington Post, Philadelphia Inquirer, MarketWatch,* CNBC, CNN, Fox Business.

Crisafulli, Patricia. *House of Dimon: How JPMorgan's Jamie Dimon Rose to the Top of the Financial World.* New York: John Wiley & Sons, 2009.

JPMorgan Chase, Annual Reports, 2014–18.

McDonald, Duff. *Last Man Standing: The Ascent of Jamie Dimon and JPMorgan Chase.* New York: Simon & Schuster, 2009.

Other Persons

Dayen, David. "Special Investigation: The Dirty Secret Behind Warren Buffett's Billions." *The Nation,* February 15, 2018.

Demos, Telis. "Robert Rubin's Legacy Up for Debate Ten Years After Citigroup Bailout." *Wall Street Journal,* June 8, 2018.

Keefe, Patrick Radden. "Carl Icahn's Failed Raid on Washington." *The New Yorker,* August 28, 2017.

Langley, Monica. *Tearing Down the Walls: How Sandy Weill Fought His Way to the Top of the Financial World and Then Nearly Lost It All.* New York: Simon & Schuster, 2003.

Stevens, Mark. *King Icahn: The Biography of a Renegade Capitalist.* New York: Dutton, 1993.

THE COMMON GOOD

Robert B. Reich makes a powerful case for the expansion of America's moral imagination. Rooting his argument in common sense and everyday reality, he demonstrates that a common good constitutes the very essence of any society or nation. Societies, he says, undergo virtuous cycles that reinforce the common good as well as vicious cycles that undermine it, one of which America has been experiencing for the past five decades. This process can and must be reversed. But first we need to weigh the moral obligations of citizenship and carefully consider how we relate to honor, shame, patriotism, truth, and the meaning of leadership. Powerful, urgent, and utterly vital, this is a heartfelt missive from one of our foremost political thinkers.

Philosophy

SAVING CAPITALISM
For the Many, Not the Few

Leading political economist Robert B. Reich presents a paradigm-shifting, clear-eyed examination of a political and economic status quo that no longer serves the people, exposing one of the most pernicious obstructions to progress today: the enduring myth of the "free market" when, behind the curtain, it is the powerful alliances between Washington and Wall Street that control the invisible hand. Laying to rest the specious dichotomy between a free market and "big government," Reich shows that the truly critical choice ahead is between a market organized for broad-based prosperity and one designed to deliver even more gains to the top. Visionary and acute, *Saving Capitalism* illuminates the path toward restoring America's fundamental promise of opportunity and advancement.

Economics

AFTERSHOCK
The Next Economy and America's Future

When the nation's economy foundered in 2008, blame was directed almost universally at Wall Street bankers. But Robert B. Reich, one of our most experienced and trusted voices on public policy, suggests another reason for the meltdown. Our real problem, he argues, lies in the increasing concentration of income at the top, robbing the vast middle class of the purchasing power it needs to keep the economy going. This thoughtful and detailed account of the American economy—and how we can fix it—is a practical, humane, and much-needed blueprint for rebuilding our society.

Current Affairs/Economics

BEYOND OUTRAGE
What Has Gone Wrong with Our Economy and Our Democracy, and How to Fix It

America's economy and democracy are working for the benefit of an ever-fewer privileged and powerful people. But rather than just complain about it or give up on the system, we must join together and make it work for all of us. In this timely book, Robert B. Reich argues that nothing good happens in Washington unless citizens are energized and organized to make sure Washington acts in the public good. The first step is to see the big picture. *Beyond Outrage* connects the dots, showing why the increasing share of income and wealth going to the top has hobbled jobs and growth for everyone else, undermining our democracy; caused Americans to become increasingly cynical about public life; and turned many Americans against one another. He also explains why the proposals of the "regressive right" are dead wrong and provides a clear roadmap of what must be done instead. *Beyond Outrage* outlines a plan of action for everyone who cares about the future of America.

Current Affairs/Economics

SUPERCAPITALISM

*The Transformation of Business,
Democracy, and Everyday Life*

From one of America's foremost economic and political thinkers comes a vital analysis of our new hypercompetitive and turbocharged global economy and the effect it is having on American democracy. With his customary wit and insight, Reich shows how widening inequality of income and wealth, heightened job insecurity, and corporate corruption are merely the logical results of a system in which politicians are more beholden to the influence of business lobbyists than to the voters who elected them. Powerful and thought-provoking, *Supercapitalism* argues that a clear separation of politics and capitalism will foster an enviroment in which both business and government thrive by putting capitalism in the service of democracy, and not the other way around.

Business

ALSO AVAILABLE

The Future of Success

Locked in the Cabinet

Reason

The Resurgent Liberal

Tales of a New America (eBook Only)

The Work of Nations

VINTAGE BOOKS
Available wherever books are sold.
www.vintagebooks.com